the homemade home

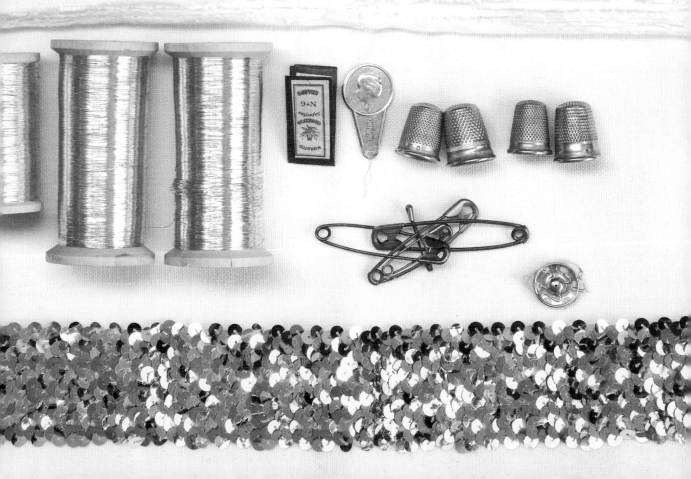

the homemade home

50 thrifty and chic
handmade projects

Sania Pell

CICO BOOKS
LONDON NEW YORK

This book is dedicated with love to my
husband Mark, and children Luke and Leila.

Published in 2010 by CICO Books
an imprint of Ryland Peters & Small
519 Broadway, 5th Floor, New York NY 10012
20–21 Jockey's Fields, London WC1R 4BW

www.cicobooks.com

10 9 8 7 6 5 4 3 2

A CIP catalog record for this book is
available from the Library of Congress and
the British Library.

ISBN-13: 978 1 907030 19 2

Printed in China

Editor: Alison Wormleighton
Design: Barbara Zuñiga
Photography: Penny Wincer
Illustration: Trina Dalziel and Stephen Dew

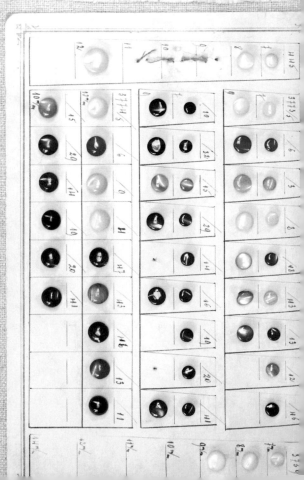

contents

introduction

There is nothing like the feeling you get when someone says how lovely something is that you are wearing, have in your home, or have given as a gift and you can reply, "I made it." This book is about making it yourself—getting creative, injecting your personality into the objects that surround you, and putting your own individual stamp on your home. It's not about difficult techniques, skills needed, or hard work, but simply trying things out, having fun, and celebrating the imperfection that comes with making things by hand.

Whether you already love making things or you haven't attempted anything since you were at school, the aim of this book is to inspire you to try. I have created some simple projects that will build the confidence of complete beginners and other projects that are more involved and require a little experience. The great thing is that they can all be made for next to nothing, using hand-me-downs, fabric scraps, leftover paint, junk shop finds, or mass-produced items. By being selective in your materials and colors you can create things that cost little but look amazing.

Become a magpie. Hoard broken jewelry, pretty buttons and trimmings, and unusual fabric remnants that could perk up a run-of-the-mill item and make it unique. Look out for items like these at thrift stores and flea markets, and snap them up even if you can't think of a use for them straightaway.

My love for making, sewing, and painting began when I was very little. My mother still uses a little felt pincushion that I made when I was six, and a lot of things we have around our own house have been made or customized by my children, my husband, or myself over the years. I hope some of the ideas in this book will help you to create your own special family keepsakes and will serve as a starting point for coming up with your own ideas for creating a wonderful, unique, homemade home.

the kitchen table

The kitchen, and especially the table around which family and friends gather for meals, is the heart of today's home. This chapter shows you how to turn mundane, functional items for the table into statement pieces that will brighten up not only your table but the entire kitchen.

appliquéd
table linen

The idea for this project started with a selection of old linen napkins in my kitchen drawers at home. The napkins were all looking a little tired, and because some had been used and laundered more than others, they were slightly different shades. There was also the odd stubborn stain that needed covering. The use of appliqué neatly solved both these problems, making a virtue of necessity, and the embroidery added color and charm. If you have more napkins than you need, you could incorporate one or two of them into the appliqué, as I've done for the flower pot on the placemat; this will help tie the various fabrics together visually.

materials

Fusible web and iron

Assortment of fabric scraps

Pen, scissors, and pins

Plain fabric placemats

Embroidery needle and floss

Carpenter's square (set square)

Napkins

Fine ribbon

Buttons, needle, and sewing thread

placemat

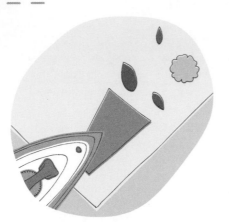

1 Following the manufacturer's directions, iron the fusible web to the wrong side of the fabric scraps you will be appliquéing to the placemat. Using the templates on page 186, draw the pot, leaves, and flowers on the paper backing of the fusible web, or draw your own designs on it. Cut out the shapes and peel off the backing paper. Arrange the shapes, right side up, on the right side of the placemat, and iron them on. For some flowers, iron a smaller flower shape, in a different color, onto a larger one.

2 Embroider the plant stem using simple running stitch (see page 160, step 2). Embroider the veins of the leaves in running stitch and the center of each flower with a French knot (see page 160, step 3) surrounded by straight stitches. Add French knots to the flower pot. Complete the placemat with running stitch around the edge in a contrasting color.

napkin

1 Iron the fusible web to the fabrics for the cupcake or the plate of strawberries. Use the templates on page 186 to draw the shapes (simply drawing a circle for the plate). Cut them out, removing the backing, and iron them to the napkin. Embroider running stitch along the cupcake case for the folds, or around the edge of the plate. Treat the strawberries as for the napkin ring, step 4.

2 To embroider the bee, split the floss in half and embroider the shape using satin stitch (see page 1600, step 2) in varying sizes to build up the shape. Start with the brown body, next embroider the yellow stripes, and then do the wings. Finally, embroider the legs and antennae using backstitch (see page 113, step 3).

napkin ring

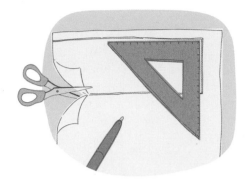

1 Cut a strip of fabric 8 x 3¼in (20 x 8cm) exactly on the straight grain. Use a carpenter's square (set square) or the corner of a book to make sure it is square. Fray the ends by teasing out the threads parallel to them using a pin.

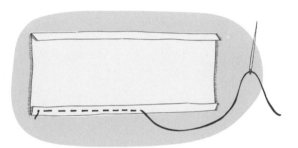

2 Turn under ¼in (5mm) on each long edge; press. Hand sew this in place using running stitch with contrasting embroidery floss.

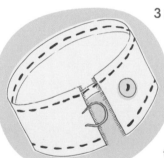

3 Sew the button to one end of the ring. Thread fine ribbon through an embroidery needle and knot one end. At the other end of the napkin ring, bring the needle up from the wrong side and insert it back through the fabric, leaving a loop. Knot this end of the ribbon on the wrong side so that the loop is just big enough to fit around the button.

4 Iron the fusible web to the fabrics for the strawberry, use the templates on page 186 to draw the shapes, and then cut them out. Iron the shapes to the center of the napkin ring. Embroider the veins of the leaves in running stitch, and add French knots to the fruit for the seeds.

storage jar labels

Dress up your storage jars with these pretty labels, made from air-hardening modeling clay, which doesn't have to be fired. They are not only decorative but practical as well. The labels are written on in pencil, so you can erase the writing and drawings and update them as the contents of the storage jars change. Use a variety of labels in different shapes and sizes on each jar, creating some of the shapes with cookie cutters. Flowers, hearts, and stars look great in combination with the simpler shapes and rectangles, all tied to the jars with pretty ribbon. You can also add decoration to the labels, in the form of textural effects or buttons.

materials and equipment

Air-hardening white modeling clay

Pastry board and rolling pin

Plastic wrap (clingfilm)

Lace, leaves, or flowers (optional)

Acrylic paint (optional)

Sharp knife and cookie cutters

Skewer or tapestry needle

Buttons and craft glue (optional)

Plastic bag

Emery board or fine sandpaper

Ribbon and lace trim

Pencil

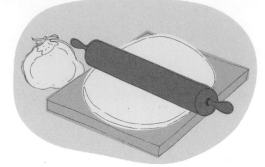

1 Begin by rolling out a piece of the clay on a pastry board using a rolling pin; keep the rest in plastic wrap (clingfilm) until needed. Roll the piece of clay out until it is approximately ⅛in (2–3mm) thick.

2 If you want to add texture, place a piece of lace, a leaf, or a flower on the clay just before doing the final rolling out. (If you wish, lightly paint the leaf first with acrylic paint, and lay it on the clay paint side down before doing the final rolling out of the clay, in order to leave a hint of color in the leaf impression in the clay. Any paint that splodges out can be removed when it is dry, in step 6.) After rolling the clay out, peel back the lace, leaf, or flower to reveal the texture.

3 With a sharp knife, cut the clay into squares and rectangles. Use cookie cutters to cut out flower or other shapes.

4 While the clay is still wet, use a skewer or tapestry needle to make a hole at the top all the way through the clay—the hole needs to be big enough to thread your ribbon through. If you want to decorate the shapes with buttons, press these into the clay while it is still wet.

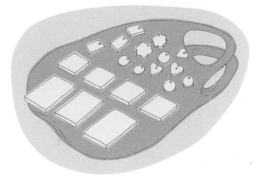

5 Carefully peel the clay shapes off the pastry board and place them on a smoothed-out plastic bag to dry. Flip the clay over every few hours to help both sides to dry evenly.

6 When the clay is dry take the shapes outdoors and, using an emery board or fine sandpaper, rub away the rough edges.

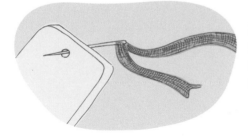

7 Thread pieces of ribbon, lace trim; or wire through the holes, with the help of a needle if the holes are small, or by just poking the ribbon through. Add as many labels as you like to the ribbon.

8 If necessary, use glue to secure any buttons you've added. Write or draw on the labels with pencil to indicate the contents of each jar.

quick idea napkin rings

look out for beautiful old buckles at flea markets and thrift stores, and put them to good use as napkin rings. Each one will be individual, whether it is made from diamanté and silver, Bakelite, or brass. Simply choose some ribbon that is the right width to fit through the buckle, slide it through (piercing a hole in the ribbon if necessary), and tie the ribbon in a bow at the back. Cut a V-shape into the center of each end of the ribbon to give it a professional finish.

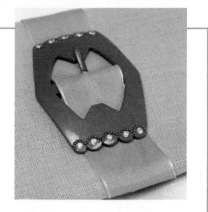

if you want to make napkins to coordinate with the napkin rings, cut 22in (55cm) squares from fabric. Turn under and press a double ½in (12mm) hem on all four edges of each square, pin, and machine stitch.

quick idea china transfers

here's the perfect way to display your children's artwork. Transfer paper such as Lazertran allows you to transfer images permanently onto glazed ceramics and then "fix" the images by baking the ceramics in your oven. You can even wash the item afterward, though not in the dishwasher. (The technique can also be used if you varnish the ceramics afterward rather than baking them—for example, for a ceramic candleholder, which couldn't be put in the oven because the candle would melt—but the design will not be as durable.)

copy all of your images onto a sheet of paper the same size as your transfer paper, so that you don't waste any. The images will be the mirror image of the final design. Ask a print shop to lazer copy it onto the transfer paper. At home, following the manufacturer's directions, cut out each design, soak it in water until the transfer loosens from the backing sheet, then slide it face down onto the ceramic. Remove any air bubbles with your fingers

fix the design by baking the ceramic in the bottom of your oven at the lowest temperature possible for at least an hour, then very gradually increasing the temperature every quarter of an hour, up to a maximum of 400°F (200°C/gas mark 7) after two hours, until the image becomes shiny, like a glaze—the longer you take, the better it will look.

quick idea teacup plants

here is a novel way to display old china that may have chips, hairline cracks, or missing handles but that is too pretty or well loved to throw away. What's more, it is on display all the time rather than just being occasionally brought out when you have a cup of tea. You can mix colors, sizes, patterns, and styles of china—the more eclectic the collection, the better it looks. Because the china does not have drainage holes in the bottom, it's important to plant only cacti or succulents in the teacups, as these plants need less watering than others.

to provide a bit of drainage, put a few small pebbles or a layer of fine gravel in the bottom, then add some suitable soil or compost on top. Place your plant on top of that, with the top of its soil a little below the top of the cup. Add more soil around the sides, keeping the plant in the center. Do not add more soil on top of the plant's existing soil. Compact the soil a little with your fingers. If you wish, sprinkle some glitter or beads on top to partially cover the soil. Do not overwater the plants.

window

In this chapter you'll discover not only how to make your own quirky curtains in ncxt to no time, but also how to enliven run-of-the-mill ready-made curtains and shades with simple add-ons, ranging from colorful pockets to graphic stripes.

curtain with pockets & flowers

Plain curtains can be transformed by sewing on decorative panels and pockets to store small, lightweight things. I also included a panel that I machine-embroidered, but you can get a similar effect without any embroidery, just by rummaging through your fabric scraps and choosing a selection of colors and prints that look good together. Some of the scraps were small and so became little pockets, while others were relatively large. I also incorporated buttons and a vintage fabric corsage.

materials and equipment

Plain curtain or pair of curtains

Long ruler and pencil

Carpenter's square (set square)

Fabric scraps and remnants

Scissors or pinking shears

Pins

Iron (optional)

Sewing machine with machine embroidery settings (optional)

Machine embroidery thread (optional)

Tape measure

Needle and sewing thread

Buttons and fabric/ribbon flowers

Ribbons

1 Place one curtain on a clean floor—it will need to be quite a large space so you can open the curtain right out. Plan your design by placing fabric scraps roughly where you would like to position the panels and pockets. If you are making a pair of curtains, begin with one curtain and then when it is completed start the next, balancing out the colors and positions of panels.

2 Using a long ruler, pencil, and carpenter's square (set square), draw a rectangle of the desired size on the wrong side of each scrap of fabric, being careful to make the edges exactly parallel to the threads. Cut out with scissors (if you want frayed or hemmed edges) or pinking shears.

3 On the pockets or panels that you haven't cut with pinking shears, fray the edges by teasing out the threads parallel to them using a pin. (Or you could turn under and press a hem all around the pockets and panels to neaten them, and then stitch the top hem of the pockets; there's no need to stitch any of the other hems because they will be stitched down in step 6.) The frayed edges add a textured effect.

4 If you want to include a machine-embroidered panel, put the embroidery foot on the machine and set the machine to "darning." This stops the machine from guiding the fabric and allows you to move it freely to create the design. Use the same color thread in the bobbin and for the top spool to give a good intensity of color. Stitch a small running stitch or small zigzag, building up the shapes slowly and carefully by stitching on top or very close to existing stitches. If you prefer, you can lightly pencil the design on the fabric beforehand, but I prefer to embroider freehand. With a little practice it is as easy as drawing on paper.

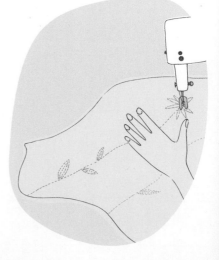

5 For any panels that have pockets stitched on top of the actual panel, stitch the pocket to the panel along the sides and bottom of the pocket, either by hand (using running stitch or backstitch) or by machine. (Similarly, for any panels stitched on top of a pocket, stitch the panel to the pocket along all four edges of the panel.)

6 Pin the panels and pockets in position on the curtain, using a tape measure to make sure the edges are parallel to those of the curtain, so they don't look crooked. I was lucky with these curtains as there was a slight stripe running through the fabric which I used as a guide. Stitch pockets to the curtain along the side and bottom edges, leaving the top open, and stitch panels to the curtain along all four edges, either by hand (using running stitch or backstitch) or by machine.

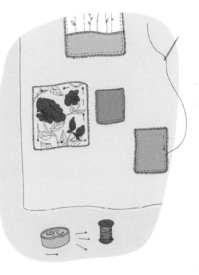

7 If there are any gaps that need filling, sew on buttons and flowers by hand.

8 Pin ribbons in place on some of the tab tops, allowing the long ends to hang down. Pin some more ribbons down the sides of the curtains. If you don't have enough ribbon to run the whole way down, you can mix it up—I think this adds charm. Stitch the ribbons to the tab tops and down the sides by hand or machine. If you have any ribbons left over, you could tie them to the top of the pole (at the outside so as not to interfere with opening and closing the curtains) or to the tabs.

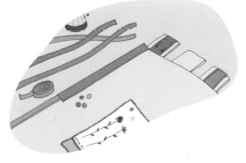

butterfly curtains

Huge butterflies that look as though they have just flown in the window and alighted on your curtains will bring a smile to anyone's face when waking up or walking into the room. The curtains themselves are not difficult to make—they are just lengths of fabric cut to size with the edges frayed. They are attached to the poles with café clips, so almost no sewing is required, but you need to choose a lightweight fabric. Most of the butterflies are cut from cotton organdy, with sequins added for a touch of glamour. However, a few butterflies are cut from sequined fabric. This fabric can be expensive so you'll probably want to cut just a few, but the solid sequin shapes do add a luxurious touch. The light bounces off them differently and sends little sparkles throughout the room.

materials and equipment

Tape measure, pencil, and scissors

Lightweight curtain fabric and pole

Iron and sewing machine

Pins, needle, and sewing thread

Paper, for butterfly patterns

Organdy, for butterflies

Sequined fabric

Sequins (loose), in various sizes

Strips of sequins

Café clips

Ribbon (optional)

1 For the length of each curtain, measure the distance from the curtain pole to the floor and then add about 12in (30cm) to allow for the fabric to puddle onto the floor. If you plan to hem the top and bottom of each curtain, allow about 2in (5cm) more.

2 For the approximate width of each curtain, measure from the end of the pole to the center, and multiply this distance by between 1½ and 3, depending on how much fullness you want. If the resulting measurement is wider than the fabric, you will need to stitch two widths together. Mark and cut out the fabric to the desired size. If necessary, pin two widths with right sides together and stitch a ⅝in (1.5cm) seam; press the seam open.

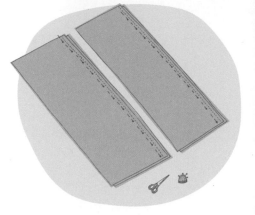

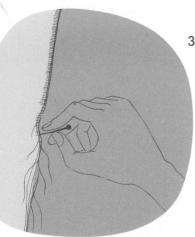

3 Because the side edges have a natural selvedge, they do not need hemming. (However, if you don't like the printing on the selvedge, you could cut it off and then treat the side edges as for the top and bottom edges.) If you want to hem the top and bottom of the fabric, turn under and press 1in (2.5cm) on the top and bottom edges; machine stitch. Alternatively, do as I did and just fray these edges, by using a pin to tease out and remove some of the threads parallel to the edge.

4 Using the templates on page 191, trace several shapes of butterflies in different sizes on paper. To make them symmetrical, cut out only half (in other words, one side) of each shape from the paper. Fold the organdy as shown, place the patterns on the organdy with the straight line on the fold of the organdy, pin in place, and cut out through both layers of the organdy.

5 Fold over some more of the organdy, and continue until you have about ten butterflies per curtain, or more if you want to layer two or three butterflies on top of each other to create the illusion of flapping wings. Also cut a few butterflies out of sequined fabric. It's easier to cut this fabric one layer at a time, so make a whole paper pattern for these, and do not fold the fabric.

6 Lay the curtains on a clean work surface, and experiment with the positioning of the butterflies on them. I placed some so they overlapped, and some to look as though they were flying off the fabric. I also occasionally pinned two or three together. When you are happy with the effect, pin them in place.

7 Stitch up the center of the organdy butterflies, and continue beyond the shape to create antennae on the curtain. You can do this either by machine (using the embroidery foot if you have one) or by hand using running stitch. The stiffness of the organdy means that you need to stitch only the centers. However, stitch each sequined-fabric butterfly all the way around its edge, otherwise it will sag under its own weight, as the sequin fabric is not stiff like the organdy.

8 Sew individual sequins onto the tops of the organdy wings and through the curtain fabric, to hold them in place. Sew strips of sequins intermittently down the leading edges (the edges that meet in the center) with stitches every ⅜in (1cm) or so. Clip the café clips to the top edge of each curtain and hang from the pole. If you wish, tie some ribbons to the clips to stream down and add extra detail.

embroidered window panel

This pretty organdy curtain panel not only gives privacy while letting in the light, but also replaces the view in or out with a striking floral design. I've used machine embroidery and appliqué to create a line of stylized flowers, as though they were growing in a window box. I love organdy's crisp, papery feel, and the delicacy of the machine embroidery is perfect for it, especially with the light flooding through. You can play on this effect with the appliqué. Contrast a delicate floral fabric, which becomes sheer at the window, with a heavier fabric that blocks out the light. However, because everything shows through and because the curtain is visible from both sides, you do have to be very neat at the back as well as the front.

materials and equipment

1 thin dowel 2in (5cm) longer than the finished width of the panel

1 thin dowel ½in (12mm) shorter than the finished width of the panel

White paint and paintbrush (optional)

Tape measure, scissors, and pencil

Sheer fabric (I used cotton organdy)

Scraps of assorted fabrics (I used prints, felt, plain linen, and leather)

Sewing machine with machine embroidery settings

Cotton machine embroidery thread in a dark color

Needle, sewing thread, and pins

Iron

Awl (bradawl)

2 small cup hooks, to fit dowel

1 Paint the two dowels white if necessary and leave to dry. Decide whether you would rather have the fabric panel just covering the glass or overlapping the wood at the top and bottom, and then measure the window. Add an extra 4in (10cm) to the width and an extra 8in (20cm) to the length, to allow for the hems and the ruching effect of the embroidery. Lay your fabric out flat on a clean floor or large work surface. Measure and cut it out.

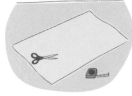

2 Find a picture of the flowers you want to copy, and keep it handy to refer to. Roughly plan out your design, remembering to allow for hems on all edges. You can lightly pencil in the design if you prefer. Some of the flowers and leaves can be just stitching, and others can incorporate fabric scraps beneath the stitching. Cut out leaf, berry, and flower shapes from the fabric scraps. To make three-dimensional flower heads from the thinner fabrics, cut out a round flower shape like an open daisy and fold it in on itself, so it forms a thin wedge at the bottom and a thicker, frilly edge at the top.

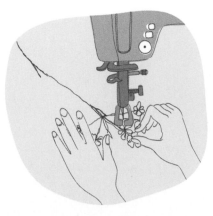

3 Thread your sewing machine with a dark embroidery thread, using the same color for the top thread and the bobbin. Put the embroidery foot on the machine and set the machine to "darning." Starting on one side of the panel, stitch the stems up from the bottom, using running stitch or small zigzag stitch. As you go, you can also stitch the leaves and flowers that will not have any fabric. Play with the size of the stitches—if you put your foot down fast on the pedal and feed the fabric through quickly, the stitches will be loose and sketchy. If you press the pedal gently and feed the fabric through slowly, they will be neat and controlled. Every now and again, check that the stems are still reasonably straight. A little crookedness adds character but too much just looks wrong.

4 Pin the fabric shapes for the berries, leaves, and flower heads to the front or back of the fabric, depending on the effect you want. (I pinned the linen leaves to the front, and the print leaves to the back.) You can also pin identical shapes to the front and back, one behind the other, for denser color. Stitch the berries and flat flower heads to the panel just inside the edge. Do the same for the leaves, but also stitch one or more lines as veins. Stitch the three-dimensional flower heads in place using straight lines fanning out from the base, like sepals.

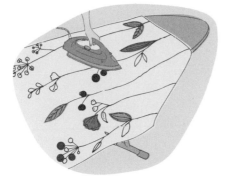

5 Iron your finished panel to flatten the stems as much as possible, but avoid flattening the three-dimensional flower heads. Measure and mark out the panel again, allowing an extra 1½in (4cm) on the width and 4in (10cm) on the length. Trim the fabric if necessary. Change the machine setting to normal, and change to the zigzagging presser foot. Zigzag stitch the raw edges that are not on the selvedge.

6 Turn under and pin a ¾in (2cm) single hem on each side and a 2in (5cm) single hem on the top and bottom. Change the machine setting from darning to normal, and change to your regular presser foot. Stitch all four hems close to the turned-under raw edge.

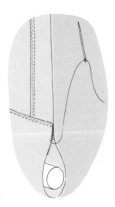

7 Slot the shorter dowel through the bottom casing, and slipstitch the side edges of the casing so that it won't slide out.

8 Slot the longer dowel through the top casing, so it extends beyond the panel by about 1in (2.5cm) at each side. Mark on the wooden window frame where the two cup hooks will need to be screwed in. Use an awl (bradawl) to make a small hole in the wood for each one, then screw in the hooks. Hang the dowel on the cup hooks.

graphic window shade decoration

The graphic quality of tape measures has always appealed to me, and here they make an interesting addition to some striped decoration, formed by assorted polka-dot ribbons, on a window shade. The additional detail of hanging keys and buttons ensures that the shade becomes quirky and intriguing, especially if you choose interesting old keys with strong silhouettes. I used a Roman shade but a roller shade could be substituted. When designing the decoration, work out how much of it you would like to be visible, because on a Roman shade the bottom part folds up first when the shade is pulled up. (If you use a roller shade, this will not be a problem.)

materials and equipment

Roman shade (or a roller shade)

Fabric tape measures

Ribbons, for decorative trim

Scissors and pins

Sewing machine

Needle and sewing thread

Buttons and keys

Narrow ribbon, for hanging keys

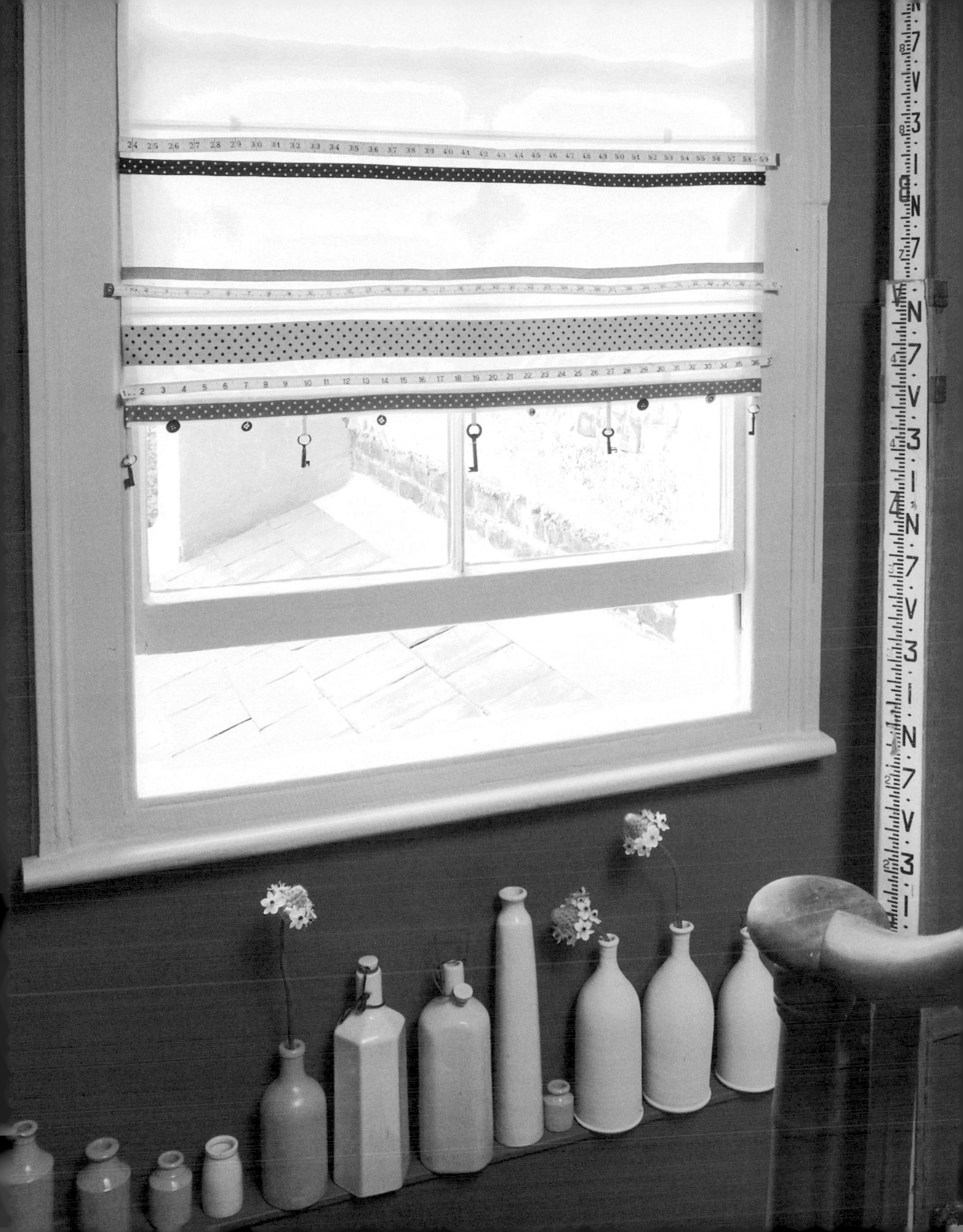

1 Lay the shade on a clean surface, either the floor or a large table, and play around with the position of the tape measures and ribbon until you are happy with how it looks. Pin and cut the ribbon and tape measures to the width of the shade plus 1½in (4cm).

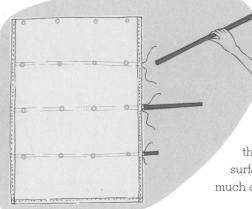

2 Unthread the string mechanism, making a mental note of how to thread it back up afterward. If you think you may forget, photograph it or draw a little diagram to remind yourself. Remove the slats from the shade if you can. You may need to unpick the stitching at the sides of the pockets and sew them up again later. I must admit I did not remove them but it made the stitching quite tricky. If you do not remove them, you will have to have plenty of space on the work surface behind your machine to pass the shade through—as much as the width of the shade.

3 Pin and machine stitch the tape measures and lengths of ribbon in place. Don't worry if they are a little crooked—it adds charm and emphasizes the handmade quality. Use the seams already in the shade as a stitching guide and avoid stitching over them, as the rods will need to be passed through again after stitching. At the sides of the shade, fold over the ends of the tape measures and ribbons to the back of the shade, and sew in place, being careful not to sew through the metal tips on the tape measures. (I actually left the ends with the metal tips visible at the front, as I liked them.)

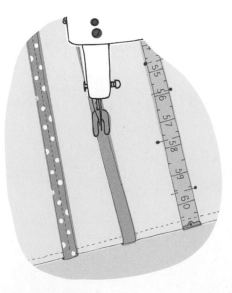

4 Sew buttons to the bottom edge of the shade. These are not sewn on in the usual way, as they hang down—you can just insert the needle and thread through one of the holes in each button, but be sure to sew them securely to the shade.

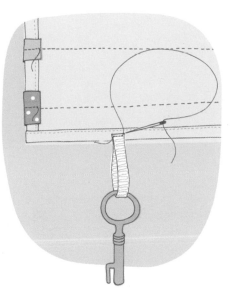

5 To attach the keys, thread some ribbon through them and hand sew or machine stitch the ends of the ribbon to the back of the shade.

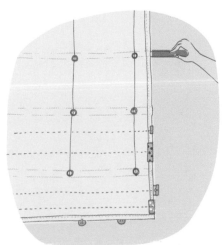

6 Rethread the string through the shade mechanism, pass the slats through the pockets in the shade, and sew up the sides of the pockets if you removed the slats previously.

seating

You don't have to reupholster your seating to give it a new lease on life. Here you will learn ingenious ways, including simple appliqué and stenciling, to create beautiful pillows and throws, turn a tired old chair into a dramatic focal point, and even update an old deck chair and footstool.

appliqué pillow

These decorative pillows can be made from scratch or by using existing pillows that need a revamp. They look great grouped together: large with small, long with tall, dark with pale—you get the gist. Jumble them up in all shapes and sizes. The flowers take very little fabric. Here I used suedette and suiting felt in different colors as it doesn't ravel. A scattering of sequins increases the glamour quotient, making the pillow sparkle when they catch the light. I used machine embroidery to create the detail of the stamens in the flower centers, as well as some of the leaf veins, but you could embroider them by hand if you prefer. The method used for making the pillow cover is the simplest there is, as it doesn't require a zipper or buttonholes. Instead, it uses an "envelope" closure.

materials

Pillow form (pad)

Fabric for pillow cover

Tape measure and long metal ruler

Pencil or tailor's chalk

Carpenter's square (set square)

Scissors, paper, and pins

Scraps of fabric to make flowers, such as suedette and suiting felt

Sewing machine

Machine embroidery thread

Embroidery needle and silver floss

Sewing needle and thread

Sequins

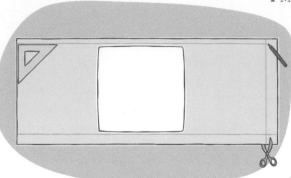

1 Measure the pillow form (pad), and mark out a rectangle on the fabric. I use a long metal ruler and a pencil or tailor's chalk, plus a carpenter's square (set square), or the corner of a book or magazine, to make sure it is square. The dimensions should be the length (from top to bottom) of the pillow form plus 1¼in (3cm), and twice the width of the pillow form plus 6in (15cm). However, if you are using a non-raveling fabric like suedette or felt, the width needs to be twice the width of the pillow form plus only 4in (10cm), rather than 6in (15cm), because you won't have to hem the edges on the opening. Cut out the fabric.

2 Using the templates on page 187, make paper patterns for the flowers and leaves, pin them to your fabric scraps, and cut out the shapes, using a variety of sizes. Cut out more than you need, so that you have enough to allow you to experiment with their position.

3 Work out the arrangement of shapes on the pillow (the center is always a good bet for your first attempt) and then pin the shapes to the right side of the fabric. You can use the flower shapes individually or combine them like petals, with the largest layer on the bottom and the smallest on top.

4 Machine embroider the flowers and leaves in place using a mixture of straight stitch and tight zigzag stitch. For the flower centers and leaf veins use embroidery thread in a dark color on a pale flower and in a light color on a dark flower. The idea is to create contrast and emphasize the detailing.

5 Hand embroider the flower stems using a large running stitch and silver floss, creating a contrast between the machine-embroidered flowers and these hand-embroidered stems.

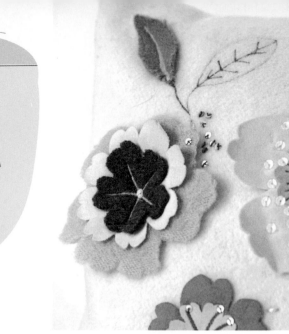

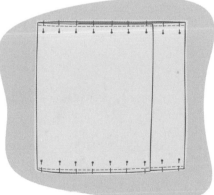

6 Hand sew sequins to the ends of the stamens, using several stitches to hold each one in position. You don't need to knot the thread and start again for each sequin, because no one will see the back.

7 If you have used a fabric that ravels, turn under and press a double ½in (12mm) hem on the raw edges that will form the opening; stitch. There is no need to do this if you have used suedette or felt. With the fabric right side up, fold the two sides in toward the center so they overlap and the width is the same as the width of the pillow form.

8 Pin the top edges and the bottom edges, right sides together, allowing for ⅝in (1.5cm) seams. Stitch the seams, snip off the corners of the seam allowances, and press the seam allowances open. Turn the cover right side out, press, and insert the pillow form through the opening.

appliqué throw

This throw is much easier to make than it looks, because it utilizes flowers cut from a print fabric and appliquéd to a base fabric. The print fabric I used was among some fabulous old remnants given to me by a friend. It must have been part of a decorator-fabric sample book as it had holes running along the top. The sequins are hiding the holes, but they add to the contemporary look I wanted to create. The gentle colors of the flowers show up well against the dark background and are livened up by flashes of bright embroidery. However, the idea would also work well with pale fabric and more subtle flowers. It's all about using the fabrics you have to create something new.

materials and equipment

Tailor's chalk, tape measure, and long ruler

Solid-color fabric, preferably with a good "drape" so it hangs well

Scissors

Iron

Fusible web

Floral fabric with motifs that can be cut out

Pins, needle, and sewing thread

Embroidery needle and floss (I used lime green and turquoise)

Sequins

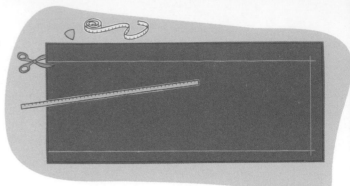

1 Using tailor's chalk, a tape measure, and a yardstick, mark the edges of the throw on the wrong side of the solid-color fabric. It needs to be long enough and wide enough to fit comfortably where you would like to drape it. Make sure all edges are straight. Cut out the fabric and press it.

2 Following the manufacturer's directions, iron fusible web onto the back of the patterned fabric. Cut out the flowers and leaves from this fabric.

3 Lay out the base fabric and spend some time arranging the cutout flowers and leaves on it, to create a new pattern. I placed mine so the flowers "grew" up the side of the throw. Also decide on the positions of the stems, which link all the flowers. You could draw them in with tailor's chalk if you wish. When you are happy with the arrangement, pin the shapes in place.

4 Starting at one end of the fabric, remove the backing paper from the flowers and leaves, and iron them on, following the manufacturer's directions and removing the pins as you go. Make sure no edges are lifting up. If you plan to wash the throw, it's a good idea to hand sew all around each one using a tiny running stitch or slipstitch.

5 Hand embroider the stems using running stitch, following the tailor's-chalk lines if you have drawn them. Embroider some leaves, too, doing the outline first in a small running stitch and then filling in the middle with small straight stitches angled to resemble the leaves' veins.

6 To finish the raw edges of the throw, hand embroider them using a combination of blanket stitch and overhand stitch. When one color ran out I simply used a contrasting one. The mixture of colors and stitches means you don't need to be too careful with your embroidery. If blanket stitch in a single color were used all the whole way around, any mistakes would be noticeable.

7 Sew on sequins where you please. I used large ones like polka dots all over the background, and small ones to disguise blemishes in the fabric and to highlight the centers of the flowers. They also add glamour.

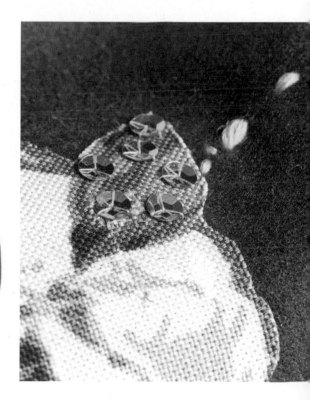

stenciled pillows

Linen gives a wonderful crispness to these pillows. With careful stenciling the bird on

the appliquéd panel should look as if it has been printed. Other simple shapes, such

as hearts, stars, letters, or numbers, could also be stenciled. The more the merrier with

pillows, as they work so well grouped together. The pillows have "envelope" closures,

which are quick and easy to make because they don't require zippers or buttonholes.

The directions overleaf are for making the bird pillow, and you can simply adapt them

for each style.

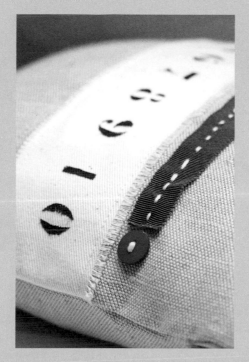

materials and equipment

Tape measure and long metal ruler

Carpenter's square (set square)

Pencil or tailor's chalk

Linen

Pillow form (pad)

Scissors, paper, and pins

Muslin (US) or calico (UK)

Cardboard for stencil

Sharp scalpel and cutting mat or
piece of thick cardboard

Acrylic fabric paint and stencil brush

Old plate and piece of paper

Ribbon and buttons

Sewing machine

Needle and sewing thread

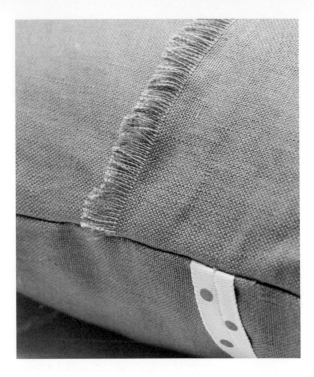

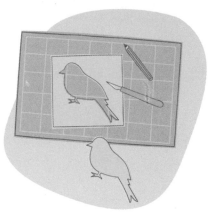

1 Mark out on the linen a rectangle twice the length of the pillow form plus 4in (10cm), and the width plus 1¼in (3cm). Cut out the linen exactly on the straight grain so that it can be frayed. Fray the two shorter edges by teasing out the threads parallel to the edge using a pin. Linen frays particularly well. Cut out a rectangle of muslin (calico) for the stenciled panel, and fray all four edges in the same way.

2 Using the bird template on page 189 or another motif of your choice, transfer the shape to a piece of cardboard. Cut it out using a sharp scalpel on a cutting mat. The stencil consists of the piece of cardboard with the central cut-out.

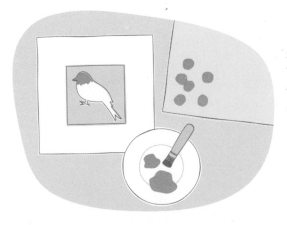

3 Put some paint on an old plate and dab the stencil brush into it. The brush should be covered but not too wet or it could leak under the stencil. Position the stencil on the muslin panel. Dab the brush on a piece of paper and, holding the stencil firmly so it won't move at all, work the paint into the panel using a dabbing action. Build up the color so it looks solid. If there is not enough coverage it will look stenciled and mottled, whereas the aim is for it to look as though it has been printed. Carefully lift off the stencil.

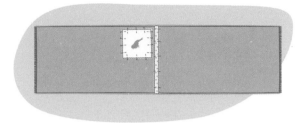

4 When the panel is completely dry, place it on the linen. The easiest way to work out the position is to wrap the fabric around the pillow form temporarily. Pin the panel to the linen. Cut the ribbon to the correct length and pin it to the linen, too, making sure it is straight. Machine stitch the panel and ribbons in place.

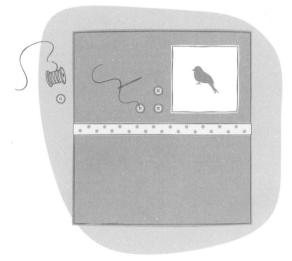

5 With the fabric right side up, fold the top and bottom in toward the center, overlapping the frayed edges of the opening, until the length is the same as the length of the pillow form. Pin the side edges together, allowing for ⅝in (1.5cm) seams. Stitch the seams, snip off the corners of the seam allowances, and press the seams open. Turn the cover right side out, press, sew on the buttons, and insert the pillow form through the opening.

quirky chair

The inspiration behind revamping this old chair came from a roll of wallpaper patterned with exotic birds, which a friend had left over from decorating her bedroom. It was perfect for creating a statement chair. I used one of the bird motifs on the top rail of the chair back (with feathers stuck on to make it even more fun) and covered the other back rail with the wallpaper. I also covered the seat with wallpaper, positioning it so there was another bird in the center (without extra feathers!). Before adding the motifs I painted the chair in bright, contrasting colors, and in addition I taped strips of patterned fabric around parts of the legs. You can get a similar effect by simply wrapping strips of fabric around the legs and tying knots to secure. With a chair like this, the more whimsical the decoration, the better.

materials and equipment

Old wooden chair

Sugar soap, sandpaper, and clean cloth

Flat latex (emulsion) paints in at least two colors and paintbrush

Paper, pencil, and scissors

Cutting mat or thick cardboard and scalpel (optional)

Wallpaper with exotic bird motif

Craft glue

Feathers in assorted sizes

Masking tape

Water-based matte varnish and brush

Double-sided tape and staple gun

Ribbon and bobble trim

Needle and thread

Fabric scraps

Sew-and-stick hook-and-loop tape such as Velcro

1 Wash the chair down with sugar soap, then sand it and wipe with a clean cloth. Apply two or three coats of paint, allowing it to dry between coats. I didn't paint the center of the seat as I would be covering it in wallpaper.

2 Place a sheet of paper larger than the seat onto the seat to make your pattern for the wallpaper. Fold it downward all the way around to create creases in the paper as a guide for cutting. Mark in pencil where to make cut-outs in the back edge for the chair back uprights. Cut out the shape of the seat along the creases. A scalpel is easier to use on the cut-outs but you can use scissors if you prefer. If it is not exact try again, because it needs to be accurate. Make patterns for the back rails in the same way.

3 Place the seat pattern over the wallpaper, centering the principal motif. Draw around the pattern with pencil and cut out the shape. Cover the chair seat in craft glue and stick the wallpaper shape down, rubbing from the center outward to get rid of air bubbles. Leave to dry. Do the same to the lower rail on the back of the chair, but make the pattern big enough to wrap right around the rail.

4 Cut out a bird or other motif from wallpaper, and trim it to fit on the top rail of the chair back. Stick some smaller feathers to the reverse of the bird using masking tape, so that the base of each feather is just poking under the wing. Spread glue on this side of the bird and stick the bird and its feathers to the rail (when gluing feathers, take care not to stick the feathery strands together). Leave to dry.

5 Apply at least two coats of varnish, using more coats on the seat to protect the paper and prevent it from ripping. Be careful not to varnish the feathers.

6 Using double-sided tape, stick ribbon all the way around the vertical edge of the seat, and then staple it for good measure. Using a needle and thread and running stitches, sew bobble trim on top of the ribbon, hiding the staples.

7 Cut the fabric scraps into strips long enough to wind around and around to cover portions of the legs, such as between the seat and the first turned ring on the leg. Stick double-sided tape to the back of the fabric strips, and wrap the strips tightly around the legs, removing the paper backing as you go. Tie a length of bobble trim to a turned ring of a chair leg, securing it with a knot. You can also tie both ends of some fabric strips in place rather than taping them if you prefer.

8 Finally, staple the large tail feathers to a strip of hook-and-loop tape. Stick a corresponding patch of the tape to the back rail of the chair under the tail feathers of the bird to make the feather tail detachable.

deck-chair and footstool covers

Worn-out deck chairs, whether languishing in your shed or picked up at a garage sale, can be given a whole new lease on life with new covers. While making them practical and sturdy, you can also go for a stylish and fun look. The fabric needs to be tough, such as the thick denim used here, and preferably without much stretch. For one deck chair and the footstool I had the dark side of the denim showing, and for the other deck chair I put the light side on top. There are also websites selling deck-chair fabric, so you can replace old stripes with new.

materials and equipment

Deck chair and footstool

Sharp craft knife

Satin eggshell paint and 2in (5cm) paintbrush

Turpentine or mineral spirits (white spirit), to clean brush

Sturdy, non-stretchy fabric such as denim

Tape measure, long ruler, and pencil

Scissors and pins

Sewing machine and sewing thread

Iron

Hammer and ⅜in (10mm) steel tacks

Small pillow forms

Heavyweight muslin (US) or calico (UK)

Scraps of fabric

Embroidery needle and floss (optional)

Leather string or ribbon for pillow

Thimble

Ribbon for footstool stripes

1 Remove the original fabric carefully, cutting it away with a sharp craft knife if necessary. Put it to one side, to serve as a pattern for the new covers. Paint the wooden part of your deck chair and footstool. After the first coat has dried, open them out to check they are fully covered. Apply a second coat, leave to dry, and then apply a third coat if necessary.

2 Measure the length of the old deck-chair cover. If you have had to cut it off the chair, add 8in (20cm) to the length. For the width, measure the narrowest part of the chair frame (usually the bottom edge), which is where the fabric will be attached, and add 2in (5cm). From the denim cut out a rectangle to these dimensions.

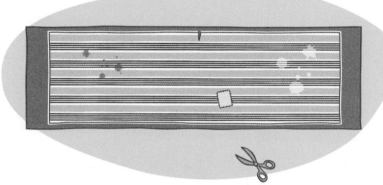

3 Zigzag stitch all four raw edges of the deck-chair cover. Turn under and press a 1in (2.5cm) hem on the two long edges, and machine stitch.

4 Try to mock up how the fabric will attach when seated before tacking it in place, to make sure it will fit. Starting at one end, nail the fabric to the underside of the wooden bar using a hammer and steel tacks. Wrap the fabric fully around the wooden bar (covering the tacks). Stretch the fabric up to the other end of the chair. Wrap this end around the bar and hammer in a couple of tacks, then check the fit. Hammer in the remaining nails.

5 Cut from the muslin a rectangle twice the length of the pillow plus 6in (15cm) and the width plus 1¼in (3cm). Using the templates on page 188, cut out apple, cherry, and leaf shapes from fabric scraps. Pin to the right side. Machine stitch or hand embroider in place. Cut out a stripe from the old cover, pin in place, and stitch. Turn under double ½in (12mm) hems on the short edges. With the fabric right side up, fold the hemmed edges in until they overlap and the cover is the length of the pillow. Pin the raw edges together and stitch ⅝in (1.5cm) seams. Snip off the corners of the seam allowances. Turn right side out; press. Insert the pillow.

6 Sew leather string or ribbon onto the top corners of the pillow. You may need to use a thimble as stitching through heavyweight fabric and leather is quite hard. Tie the pillow to the wooden frame of the deck chair.

7 To make the footstool cover, cut out your denim to the size of the old fabric that you removed in step 1, adding 2in (5cm) to the depth if it wasn't hemmed. Zigzag all edges. Turn under, press, and machine stitch a 1in (2.5cm) hem on the front and back edges. Cut out an apple shape and attach it as for the deck chair (see step 5). To create the stripes, pin the ribbon to the fabric and machine stitch.

8 Place the new cover in position over the footstool and attach the cover in the same way as the previous cover. (If your stool has wooden fixing slots, you may need to iron the sides of the new cover to flatten them and make it easier to insert them into the fixing slots.)

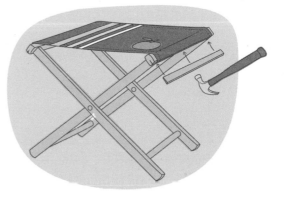

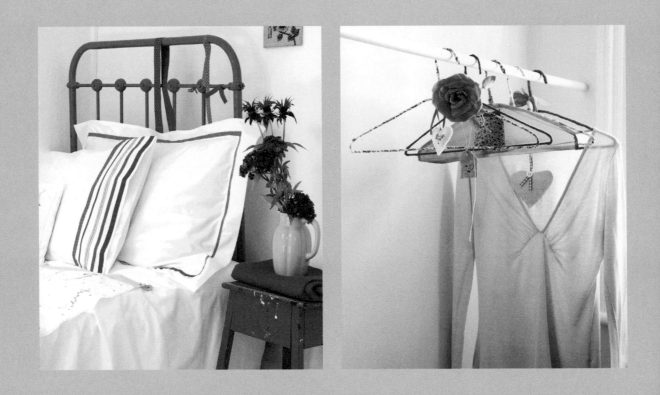

bed

The projects in this chapter will help you transform
every aspect of your bedroom. There are inspiring ideas
for brightening up your chests of drawers, embellishing
your bed linen, creating gorgeous pillows, and even
making your coat hangers so pretty that you won't
want to banish them to the closet.

embellished bed linen

Turn plain white bed linen into a beautiful and colorful bedroom feature with embroidery panels and ribbons. Stripes of brightly colored ribbon are such a great way to add interest to plain pillowcases, while the small, square pillow has a plain cover with a hand-embroidered panel sewn to the front. The duvet cover has a machine-embroidered panel buttoned onto it, which can be removed when the cover is washed. If you have an antique lace panel, a piece of vintage embroidery, or even just a beautiful, delicate piece of fabric, the small pillow or the duvet cover would be an ideal way to show it off. Or you could make your own embroidered panel using hand or machine embroidery, and then choose matching ribbons for the pillowcases.

materials and equipment

Long ruler and tailor's chalk

Scissors and pins

Sewing machine, needle, and thread

Also needed for pillowcase decoration:

Pillowcases

Small, pointy scissors

Colorfast ribbon

Also needed for duvet cover decoration:

Duvet cover

Embroidered panel, or fabric and machine embroidery thread to make your own panel

Strips of one or two other fabrics

Ribbons and four buttons

Embroidery needle and floss

standard ("housewife") pillowcase with stripes

1 Turn the pillowcase wrong side out and carefully unpick part of each side seam using small, pointy scissors, working from the open end and unpicking about 8in (20cm) of the seam. Turn the pillowcase right side out.

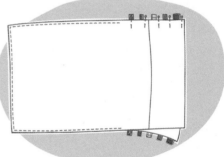

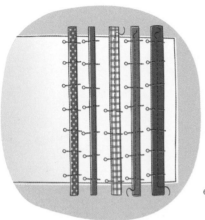

2 Cut five lengths of ribbon, each 2in (5cm) longer than the width of the pillowcase. Place them on the pillowcase and decide what spacing will look best. Using a long ruler and tailor's chalk, draw lines for the stripes on the right side of the pillowcase front. Pin the ribbons along the lines, pinning to the front only, and extending beyond the edge equally at both sides. Use enough pins to keep the ribbons straight while you are stitching. Machine stitch down the middle of each ribbon.

3 Turn the pillowcase wrong side out again, and restitch the side seams, catching the ends of the ribbons in the seams. Turn right side out.

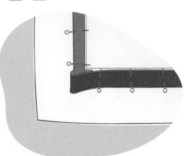

flanged ("Oxford") pillowcase with decorative border

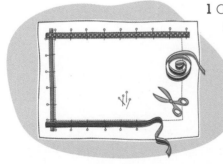

1 Cut four lengths of ribbon to fit around the flange, just outside the seams—two shorter lengths and two longer lengths, each plus 2in (5cm). Pin the ribbon along the seams.

2 At the corners, turn under the ends of the ribbons. Machine stitch the ribbons in place.

duvet cover with embroidered panel

1 If you are making the panel from scratch, cut out a piece of fabric exactly on the straight grain. Use a pin to fray all four edges by removing some of the threads parallel to the edge. For the machine embroidery, you can use a short straight stitch, a zigzag stitch, free stitching (with the embroidery foot and the machine set to "darning"—see page 165), or a combination of these. If you wish, lightly draw the design on the panel first with tailor's chalk. Use the same color thread on the bobbin and the top spool to give a good intensity of color.

2 Cut out two or three narrow strips of fabric to the width of the panel, and fray one long edge and both ends of each. Lap one end of the panel over the unfrayed edge of one strip. Pin and machine stitch together. Repeat at the other end of the panel with one or two more strips. Cut ribbons to the width of the panel plus 1in (2.5cm). Using a long ruler and tailor's chalk, mark their position on one of the strips. Turn under ½in (12mm) at each end, pin to the fabric, and machine stitch in place. If desired, hand embroider running stitch or other stitches in floss across one or more of the strips.

3 Cut four lengths of ribbon that are each long enough to loop around a button plus an extra 2in (5cm). Pin both ends of a ribbon loop to the wrong side of the top and bottom strips at each corner, adjusting the size of the loop to fit the button. To hold each loop in place, hand embroider a cross stitch through both ends of the ribbon using six strands of floss. Mark with tailor's chalk on the top of the duvet cover exactly where the corresponding four buttons will need to go in order for the panel to lie flat. Sew the buttons to the top of the cover (be careful not to sew them to the bottom of the cover as well!). Fit the loops over the buttons.

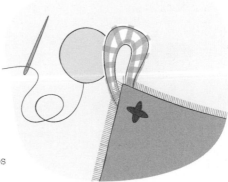

decorated
cupboard

This old cupboard looked very tired when it was first given to me, but I transformed

it using a few creative techniques. I wanted to give it a magical feel, and so the key

element is the fairytale tree that looks like it's growing over the cupboard. It consists

of a stenciled branch and leaves, with more leaves cut from wallpaper and from craft

metal and then stuck on. A few mirror disks and two door knobs covered in glitter

complete the fantasy effect. Your design does not have to stop at the furniture—it can

extend onto the wall. Here the mirror disks that I used on the cupboard are also on

the wall, but you could continue motifs cut from the wallpaper onto the wall.

materials and equipment

Old cupboard or nightstand or other piece of furniture

Sugar soap, sandpaper (optional), and clean cloth

Satin-finish water-based wood paint and paintbrush

Pencil, scalpel and cutting mat or thick cardboard

Posterboard (card) for stencil

Masking tape, old saucer, and paper

Acrylic paint and stencil brush

Wallpaper with large individual flowers and leaves to cut out

Scissors and white glue

Matte water-based varnish and brush

Sheet of craft metal and real leaves

Extra-strong multipurpose glue

Mirror disks and glitter

Door knobs

1 Wash the cupboard with sugar soap. Sand if necessary and wipe with a clean cloth. Paint with two or three coats of paint, allowing it to dry between coats.

2 With a pencil, sketch a branch shape of the appropriate size on posterboard (card). When you are happy with the design, cut the shape out using a scalpel on a cutting mat or thick cardboard. Cut out some more stencils for the leaves from separate pieces of posterboard.

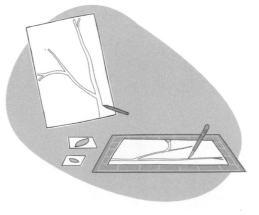

3 Lay the cupboard on its back, position the branch stencil on top, and tape it around the edges using masking tape. (If the design continues onto the top and/or side of the cupboard, part of the stencil will be unused and so will extend beyond the edge of the nightstand.) Put some acrylic paint on an old saucer and dip the stencil brush into it. Dab it on a separate piece of paper to remove any excess, leaving the brush still loaded with paint but not too wet. Start stippling paint onto the cupboard through the stencil, holding the stencil flat to the surface while you do so to keep seepage under the edges to a minimum. Build up the layers until the color is solid. Leave to dry and then remove the stencil unless you are continuing the design on the top.

4 If you are continuing the branch onto the top, stand the cupboard up, fold the stencil along the top edge of the cupboard, and tape it to the top. Stencil the top as for the front. Do the same for the side if applicable. (The previously used portion of the stencil remains taped to the front.) Remove the stencil.

5 Stencil some leaves in the same way as in step 3, leaving them to dry. Cut out wallpaper leaves and stick them on with white glue. Make sure they are covered in glue on the underside all the way to the edges, so the edges will not lift.

6 When the glue is dry, varnish the cupboard so that the wallpaper will not peel off and the stenciling will not scratch or chip off.

7 Make metal leaves by rubbing the craft metal onto a real leaf using your fingers (or rubbing it with a corner of the clean cloth if you prefer)—the impression will show through. Cut out the leaf shapes with scissors. (The little silver bird was a cut-out I already had.) When the varnish is dry, and with the cupboard lying on its back, stick on the metal leaves using extra-strong multipurpose glue. Also use this glue to stick on some mirror disks. Leave until the glue dries. (They are not varnished.)

8 Paint white glue onto the door knobs and sprinkle glitter over them, covering the knobs completely. When the glue has dried, paint the knobs with varnish to keep the glitter in place. When this is dry, screw the knobs onto the cupboard.

lovebird pillows
with silk flowers

The idea for this array of pillows started with the pair of birds, which were on an apron I found in a sale. As it cost next to nothing, I didn't feel bad about cutting it up to reuse the birds. If you can't find a suitable bird print fabric, however, you could use one with a butterfly print or something similar. The branch the birds are sitting on is appliquéd fabric, and I added some silk flowers and leaves to create the effect of spring blossom. The flower pillows are made using cutout fabric flowers on embroidered stems, and even the chintz-type fabric has some added silk flowers and leaves. Green sequins sewn onto all the pillows add a delicate sparkle.

materials and equipment

Solid-colored and floral linen, for pillow covers

Pillow forms (pads)

Scissors and pins

Long ruler, tailor's chalk, and pencil

Carpenter's square (set square)

Fusible web and iron

Patterned fabrics with flowers and birds that can be cut out

Dark fabric, for branch

Silk flowers and leaves

Embroidery needle and floss in yellow and pink

Sewing needle and sewing thread

Green sequins and yellow beads

Green embroidery floss, or sewing machine and machine embroidery thread

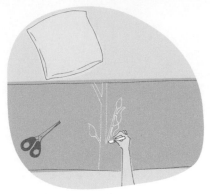

1 For each pillow cover, cut from the linen a rectangle twice the length of the pillow plus 6in (15cm) and the width plus 1¼in (3cm). Using tailor's chalk, mark the main elements of the design on the right side of each fabric piece.

2 For the bird pillow, iron fusible web to the wrong side of the bird fabric and the wrong side of the dark fabric for the branch. On the backing paper of the fusible web ironed to the dark fabric, draw a branch (remembering that it will be the mirror image of the final design). Cut it out. Also cut out the birds from the bird fabric. Remove the backing paper and iron the branch and then the birds in position on the right side of the linen.

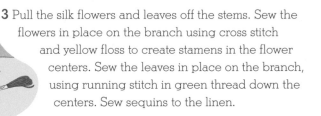

3 Pull the silk flowers and leaves off the stems. Sew the flowers in place on the branch using cross stitch and yellow floss to create stamens in the flower centers. Sew the leaves in place on the branch, using running stitch in green thread down the centers. Sew sequins to the linen.

4 For the floral-patterned pillow, sew on additional silk flowers with little yellow beads in the centers. Sew sequins to the linen.

5 For the flower pillows, embroider green vertical stems with tiny leaves either by hand using running stitch or backstitch, or by machine using zigzag stitch. You could also sew on a strip of green sequins to make a wider stem, as I did on the light-colored pillow.

6 Cut out some flowers (and leaves if you wish) from fabrics and iron fusible web to the wrong side. Remove the backing paper, and iron them to the tops of the stems. If you wish, you could use free machine embroidery to stitch over the centers and stems and to add the outline of another flower or two.

7 Pull flowers and leaves off the stem of some silk flowers, and sew the leaves to the embroidered stem using running stitch and green thread down the centers. Sew the silk flowers in clusters at the top of other embroidered stems, using cross stitch to create stamens in the centers. Sew sequins to the linen.

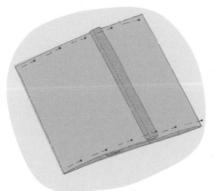

8 Complete the cover by hemming the short edges, stitching the side seams, and turning right side out, as for the pillow on page 63, step 5.

lacy bed runner

I started collecting lace when I was given some by my grandmother, who had acquired it over many years. I then augmented my collection with flea market finds and pieces cut from garments that were well past their best. For this runner, I started with some linen left over from making the bed's headboard. Onto this base fabric I stitched parallel lines of lace trimming interspersed with ribbons and sequin strips. In addition there are some strips of fabric that I painted with a lace pattern, using inexpensive lace fabric as a stencil. My favorite elements are the long, thin plackets containing buttons and buttonholes, cut from a vintage pillowcase that was no longer usable. Some of the trimmings weren't long enough to run from one side to the other, so I allowed them simply to stop short, which adds interest to the design. All this gives the runner a contemporary, quirky look. Matching pillow covers can be made from more spray-painted fabric or from the base fabric trimmed with scraps of the lace.

materials and equipment

Base fabric, such as linen

Long ruler and pencil or tailor's chalk

Scissors and pins

Assorted lengths of lace trimming

Iron

Tightly woven fabric, to be spray-painted

Old newspaper

Lace fabric, to use as stencil

Spray paint in off-white

Ribbons and sequin strips

Button/buttonhole plackets (if available)

Needle and sewing thread

1 Mark out and cut a piece of fabric that is big enough to hang down on both sides of the bed, taking care to cut exactly along the grain. Fray the edges using a pin (or, if you prefer, you could turn under a narrow hem, press, and stitch). Hand wash all the pieces of lace, and press them when dry. Press the base fabric and the fabric you will be stenciling.

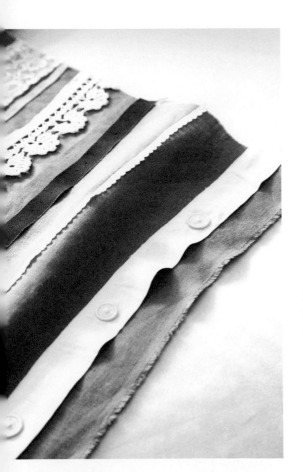

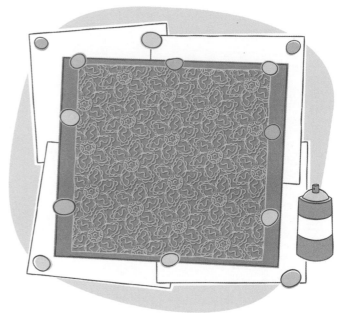

2 Place the fabric to be stenciled on some newspaper in a well-ventilated space—ideally, outdoors—holding it down with some pebbles. Position the cheap lace on top, to serve as a stencil. Make sure it is stretched taut and flat, and hold it in place with pebbles, too. Spray-paint through the lace until you have an even buildup of paint, being careful always to spray from directly above, otherwise the paint could creep under the edges of the lace design.

3 When the paint is dry, carefully peel off the lace to reveal the pattern beneath. Cut the sprayed fabric into strips, cutting exactly on the straight grain, and fray the long edges as for the base fabric in step 1.

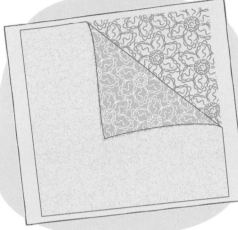

4 Lay the base fabric out flat, right side up, and pin the stenciled fabric strips, lace trim, ribbon, plackets (if available), and sequin strips to the base fabric in parallel lines, leaving about ½in (12mm) at the ends to fold over to the back. On any lengths that do not extend all the way across the runner, turn under ¼in (5mm) on the end that will be visible.

5 Hand sew the decoration to the fabric using small running stitches, sewing down the center of narrow trimming or along both edges if it is wider. Fold the ends over to the back and sew in place.

covered coat hangers

Transform wire coat hangers into pretty confections of fabric and ribbon. Start by binding the wire with strips of fabric (or you could use ribbon if it's not too narrow or flimsy). You can then decorate the bound hangers with cheerful fabric covers, felt lavender bags, or felt labels. Every time you open the wardrobe you will feel uplifted! In fact, these hangers are almost too pretty to hide in a wardrobe—you could display favorite items of clothing on them and have them hanging on display.

materials and equipment

Wire coat hangers

Double-sided tape

Pencil or tailor's chalk and long ruler

Fabric, for binding

Scissors, pins, and iron

Scraps of felt and patterned fabric, for decoration

Ribbons, buttons, large fabric corsages (see page 149, step 6, to make your own), silk flowers, or other trimmings

Needle and sewing thread

Dried lavender

Teaspoon or paper

Paper silk or other fabric that doesn't ravel easily, for cover

Sewing machine (optional)

1 To bind each hanger, first run a strip of double-sided tape along the wire, wrapping the tape over the wire so it is completely covered. Do this in sections or you will end up in a sticky mess. Using a pencil and long ruler, mark out strips 1¼in (3cm) wide on the wrong side of the fabric. They should be roughly 3ft (1m) long, but this does not have to be exact—it is simply to minimize the number of separate strips, without their being too hard to handle. Cut out the strips—about two or three strips per hanger should probably be enough. Turn under and press ¼in (5mm) on one long edge and both ends of each fabric strip.

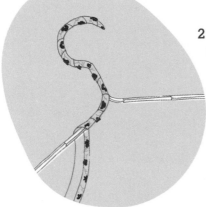

2 Remove the backing paper from the tape on the hook. Starting at the end of the hook, and with the turned-under edge of the fabric strip by the end of the hook, begin spiraling a fabric strip around the wire. The fabric will stick to the double-sided tape, and each new spiral of fabric should overlap the previous spiral, covering the raw edge. Remove the backing paper from the tape as you go. Continue in this way until the whole hanger is covered.

3 For a lavender heart, cut out two identical heart shapes from felt, and one smaller heart from a patterned fabric. Hand sew the smaller heart to one felt heart with running stitch. Pin one felt heart to the other one, wrong sides together. Fold a length of narrow ribbon in half, and insert the folded end into the pinned seam at the top of the heart; pin.

4 Hand sew the two hearts together with tiny running stitches near the edge, leaving a small opening at one side. Fill the felt heart with lavender, using a teaspoon or a funnel made from paper. Sew the opening closed using running stitch aligned with the other stitching. Tie the heart to a bound hanger and decorate the hanger with a fabric corsage.

5 For a label, cut out a label shape or a heart shape from felt. Cut out a smaller heart from patterned fabric and sew it to the felt with small running stitches. Make a hole in the top of the felt, and thread ribbon through the hole. Tie the label to a bound hanger, along with a fabric corsage, silk flowers, or other trimmings.

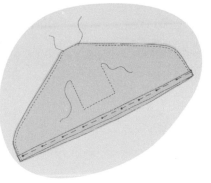

6 For a cover, place a bound hanger on the paper silk and draw around it with a pencil or tailor's chalk, omitting the hook and allowing an extra ¾in (2cm) all around. Cut out two pieces in this way. For the cover's pocket, cut out a square of patterned fabric exactly on the straight grain, and fray each edge by using a pin to remove the outer threads parallel to that edge. Pin the pocket right side up to the right side of one piece of the paper silk. Stitch by hand or machine along the side and bottom edges of the pocket.

7 Pin one cover piece to the other with right sides together. Stitch a ⅝in (1.5cm) seam by hand or machine, leaving a small opening in the seam at top center for the hook, and leaving the bottom open. Turn up a double ¼in (5mm) hem along the bottom edge of the front and back. Press and pin. Stitch the hem by hand or machine. Turn right side out and press. Sew a tiny flower to the top of the cover.

8 For the lavender parcel to go in the cover's pocket, cut two squares of contrasting fabric slightly smaller than the pocket. Pin one to the other with right sides together. Stitch a ¼in (5mm) seam by hand or machine around all four edges, leaving an opening in one side. Turn right side out and press. Fill the parcel with dried lavender and stitch the opening closed. Slip the cover over a bound hanger (or just bind the hook) and place the lavender parcel in the pocket of the cover. Tie a small ribbon around the hook.

cowboy-collage
chest of drawers

This old chest of drawers once belonged to my parents—it was the first piece of furniture they bought after getting married, transported to their new marital home on the roof of a Mini Cooper. It was originally varnished dark brown and had ornate brass handles, so I painted it and replaced the handles. The cowboy images were color-photocopied from a 1950s book I found in a thrift shop. (An alternative would be to photocopy simple images in black and white and ask the children to color them in.) Copy more images than you need, so that you have enough to play around with. To stimulate my little boy's imagination, I created scenes with the pictures. I painted the insides of the drawers in bright colors and lined the top edges with very thin ribbon, but a contrasting paint could be used instead of ribbon.

materials and equipment

Chest of drawers

Newspaper and plain paper

Medium- and fine-grade sandpaper

Clean cloth

Satin-finish water-based paint in assorted colors

2in (5cm) paintbrush

Low-tack masking tape

Thin ribbon and double-sided tape

Photocopied images

Small craft scissors and sharp scalpel

Cutting mat or thick cardboard

Putty-like adhesive

Spray glue

Water-based flat varnish and brush

1 You can paint just the chest or just the drawers, or both. Remove the drawers, placing the chest and the drawers on newspaper. Take off the handles. Sand down all surfaces with medium sandpaper and then fine sandpaper. Wipe with a dry cloth. Apply two or three coats of paint, allowing it to dry between coats.

2 Mask the edges of the drawers with masking tape to protect the painted areas and to keep the lines crisp. Paint the insides of the drawers with two or three coats of bright color(s), allowing the paint to dry between coats.

3 Carefully remove the masking tape. When the insides of the drawers are completely dry, either mask the painted areas and paint the top edges of the drawers a contrasting vibrant color, or stick thin ribbon to the top edge using double-sided tape. The ribbon should not be too thick or it may jam the drawers when you open and shut them.

4 Cut out the pictures with small craft scissors. For the tricky areas, place the picture on the cutting mat or cardboard, and cut out with a sharp scalpel.

5 Put the drawers back in the chest. Temporarily position the pictures on the drawer fronts with putty-like adhesive to give you an idea of how they will look. Adjust their positions until you are satisfied with the arrangement, remembering to allow for the handles.

6 In a well-ventilated room and working on a covered surface, take one picture, remove the adhesive, place the picture on plain paper, and spray the back well with glue. Check that the coverage is even, especially at the edges, and then place back in position. Repeat for the next picture. Continue until all the pieces are stuck on.

7 Take the drawers out again and stand them on end on the newspaper. Apply a flat clear varnish to stop the corners from peeling and allow the surface to be cleaned with a damp cloth. It also helps prevent little fingers from peeling off the pictures! When dry, put the handles back on and put the drawers back in the chest.

quick idea ribbon pulls

simply decorate the drawer pulls and you can perk up a whole chest of drawers, whether old or new. Unscrew the pulls and paint with two or three coats of paint. Use up leftover paint or sample pots, and don't worry if you don't have enough paint to make all the pulls the same—using different colors adds a fun, slightly fifties feel. When dry, put the pulls back on the drawers and decorate them further by twisting bits of old ribbon or old braid and then tying them around the pulls. Cut ribbon ends on the diagonal to prevent fraying.

make labels for each drawer by using old paint-color cards or any other leftover thin cardboard. Cut them out to the shape you want and punch a hole in the top so they can be attached to the drawers. Draw pictures on the labels to indicate the contents of the drawers, and tie them onto the pulls. You could use string or thread, but for added prettiness, use a piece of narrow ribbon in a color that matches the pull.

light

No need to covet those designer lights—the
projects in this chapter will give you lighting that
is just as eye-catching and individualistic. Whether
you use paint, felt, ribbons, buttons, beads, sequins,
diamanté, or chandelier drops, the lighting of
your home will never be the same again.

crystal lamp

Paint, wallpaper, ribbons, and chandelier droplets will transform an old, plain lamp beyond all recognition. I bought these antique droplets at a garage sale—you can often find them in flea markets and antique shops, especially where antique lighting is sold. Christmas decorations often have acrylic droplets that can be used in the same way, or pretty buttons strung together with wire (see Wired Button Decorations, page 126) would also work. I painted the lamp base and decorated the shade with the crystals and some ribbon, diamanté, rhinestones, sequins, and cutout motifs from a wallpaper sample—no need to buy a whole roll. More ribbons and strips of fabric tied or stuck around the base completed the makeover. The colors I chose echo the icy colors of the droplets.

materials and equipment

Old lamp base and shade	Ribbons and fabric scraps
Sugar soap or wet-and-dry sandpaper and clean rag	Scissors
Newspaper	Wallpaper with motifs that can be cut out
Satin eggshell paint and 1½in (4cm) paintbrush	All-purpose glue
Specialist hole-punch or awl (bradawl), small hammer, and cutting mat or thick cardboard	Diamanté and sequins
	Thin wire
Double-sided tape	Antique chandelier droplets
	Buttons

1 To create a "key" so the paint will stick, give the lamp base a quick wipe down with sugar soap, or lightly sand it with wet-and-dry paper and then wipe over it with a clean rag. Protect your work surface with plenty of newspaper and then paint the base with two or three coats of paint, allowing it to dry between coats.

2 While the base is drying, punch holes around the bottom rim of the shade. They do not have to be evenly spaced—a little random spacing is fine. I use a specialist hole-punch with a small hammer to make a hole, because it gives me more control over the positioning. An awl (bradawl) can be used in the same way but does not give as crisp a finish. Whichever you use, it must be done on a cutting mat or thick cardboard to avoid damaging the work surface.

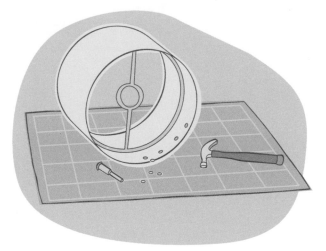

3 Attach double-sided tape to the back of a length of ribbon. To stick the ribbon to the shade, wind it carefully around the bottom of the shade just above the holes, peeling off the backing paper from the tape and smoothing out bumps as you go. Repeat for a second length of ribbon.

4 With scissors, cut out the motifs from the wallpaper, and stick them to the shade with all-purpose glue or double-sided tape. Glue diamanté and sequins to each flower.

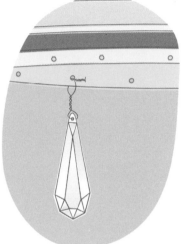

5 Thread a length of wire through the top of each crystal, twisting it to secure, and then thread it through a hole punched in the shade. Twist the ends together on the inside of the shade, where they won't be visible.

6 Cut the fabric scraps into strips and tie them and lengths of ribbon around the stem of the base, with the knots at the back. Use double-sided tape to stick a piece of ribbon around the base.

sculptural lamp

This floor lamp has had a rather dramatic transformation! The previous shade was a stained, faded green one with a sad fringe limping around the edge. It was with great pleasure that I ripped it off to reveal its bones beneath, which were much more interesting than the solid shade. I focused attention on the framework by giving it a respray and decorating it with flowers. Some of the flowers were made from scratch using felt, others were sections of a vintage velvet corsage, while still others were store-bought silk flowers that I dissected and reassembled. I also decorated the base with paint and ribbons to match the "shade." This ugly sister has been transformed into Cinderella.

materials and equipment

Lamp base and shade

Fine-grade sandpaper and clean cloth

Masking tape, newspaper, and pebbles

Eggshell paint in one color, for base

2in (5cm) paintbrush

Double-sided tape and scissors

Spray paint in two bright colors, for shade frame

Ribbon (no wider than height of vertical edge of bottom part of lamp base) in color to match spray paint

Scissors, needle, and sewing thread

Felt in assorted colors

Beads

Sequins (optional)

Ribbon in assorted colors, to decorate flowers

Vintage corsage (optional)

Silk flowers and fine wire

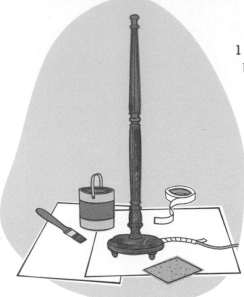

1 Remove the bulb and shade. Sand the lamp base lightly and wipe with a clean cloth. Protect the cord with masking tape near where it joins the base. Place the lamp base on sheets of newspaper, and paint it with the eggshell paint. Give it two or three coats, allowing it to dry between coats.

2 When the lamp base is completely dry, stick double-sided tape to the back of the ribbon. Remove the backing paper and stick the ribbon around the vertical edge of the bottom of the base.

3 Cut off all the fabric and any trim from the old lampshade to reveal the wire frame. Sand the frame to remove any rust or flaking paint, and then wipe with a clean cloth. Place the frame on newspaper in a well-ventilated space (ideally outdoors, holding the newspaper in place with pebbles) and spray with a bright-colored paint. Do this slowly, building up the color intensity. I used bright orange for the outer portion of the frame and shocking pink for the central support on which the shade sits. Leave to dry.

4 To make the round felt flowers, cut out flower shapes in different sizes and colors. Lay three on top of each other, with the largest on the bottom and the smallest on top. Sew them together in the center, pinching the back in a little while sewing, so that the flower is not quite flat. Sew beads or sequins to the center on the front. Sew a length of ribbon to the center of each flower on the back.

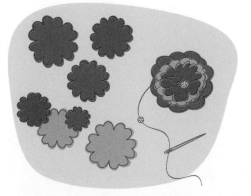

5 To make the conical felt flowers, take just one of the round flower shapes and fold it into a cone, then secure it with small running stitches running along the edge from the point to about halfway down. Sew a length of ribbon to the point of each flower on the back.

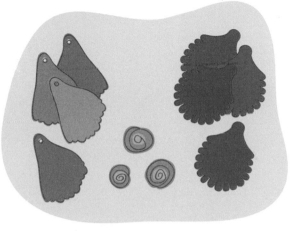

6 Separate the vintage velvet corsage (if you have one) into usable sections. Pull flowers and buds off the stems of the silk flowers and use them in new, smaller groupings or individually.

7 You can either tie the flowers to the frame with the attached ribbons, or wire them on (leaving any ribbons to hang down). To wire them, poke one end of a length of wire in and out of the flower from the back (using a needle to make a hole first if necessary) and twist around on itself to secure. Thread beads onto the wire and onto other lengths of wire, and twist to secure. Twist the wired flowers and beads onto the frame, using the beads to hide some of the wires.

8 Wrap ribbon around portions of the struts, securing with a knot to begin with and another knot at the end. Use the ribbon to hide any wire that is still visible, tucking it under the ribbon.

creepy-crawly lamp

A map showing a region that means something to a child makes a great lampshade for their bedroom, especially if you attach some fun "creepy-crawlies" to it. This one shows an area in France we visited on vacation (and got stuck in a traffic jam, hence the plastic snail). Alternatively, you could use, say, a map of the oceans, and decorate it with plastic marine creatures; or a map of the night sky, complete with pin pricks for stars which will show when the lamp is turned on, decorated with planets orbiting the shade. Or you could use a map of the Wild West, with plastic cowboys and horses hanging from the shade; a map of your town, surrounded by tiny cars and trucks; or a map of familiar countryside, with attached plastic farm animals. Involve the child in thinking up the ideas and decorations, and they will love it all the more.

materials

Newspaper and masking tape

Old lamp base and shade with sides that do not taper

Paintbrush and paint

Turpentine or mineral spirits (white spirit), to clean brushes if paint is oil-based

Matte varnish, if paint is water-based

Map

Scissors

Scalpel and metal ruler (optional)

Cutting mat or thick cardboard

Double-sided tape

Specialist hole-punch or awl (bradawl) and hammer

Plastic creatures

Thin wire

1 Cover your work surface with newspaper to protect it. Remove the shade from the lamp. Using masking tape, mask the parts of your lamp that won't be painted, such as the cord (flex) and the metal area that holds the bulb. Paint the base with two or three coats of paint, allowing it to dry between coats. If you have used water-based paint, apply a coat of matte varnish after the paint is dry.

2 Open up the map and choose the area you want to use. Roll the shade along the map and mark the map to work out the size needed, adding ½in (1cm) all around (which will be cut off later). Cut out using scissors, or a scalpel with a metal ruler and cutting mat.

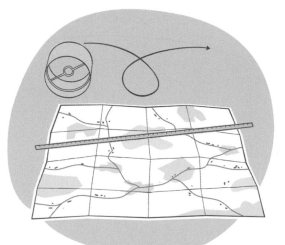

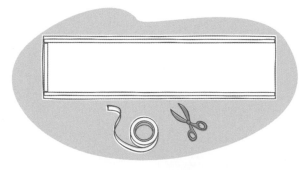

3 On the underside of the cutout map, on the two long edges and one short edge, stick double-sided tape ½in (1cm) in from the edge and parallel to it.

4 Begin sticking the map carefully to the shade, starting with the end that has the tape and peeling off the backing paper on the tape as you go. Make sure you start off straight or the map will get more out of position as you roll it around the shade. Slowly work your way around the circumference. If you begin to go off track, carefully unpeel the map and put it straight. When you are happy with how the map is positioned on the shade, cut off the excess paper with sharp scissors. Put some double-sided tape on the underside of the end of the map, remove the backing, and stick it down.

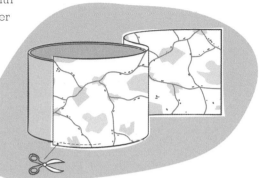

5 Lay the shade on a cutting mat or thick piece of cardboard. Punch holes around the bottom of the shade using a specialist hole-punch and hammer, which gives more accuracy than a traditional one. Or use an awl (bradawl), but this does not give as crisp a finish. Whichever you use, push against the cutting mat as you make the holes to stop the shade from creasing. The holes do not need to be evenly spaced around the shade—slightly random positioning is fine.

6 Wrap a piece of wire around each creature, hiding the wire if possible. For example, on these plastic insects it is around the thorax or legs or under the wings. Twist the wire together to hold it in place leaving the two ends free. Poke one end through one of the punched holes and twist the ends together on the inside of the shade. To secure the snail in the middle of the shade, either punch two holes close together and proceed as for the holes at the edge, or make just one hole and insert both ends of the wire through it, making a large knot on the inside right next to the shade so the ends cannot slide back through the hole.

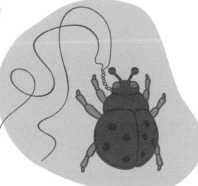

quick idea jar candle holders

these jars decorated with fabric scraps look pretty even when unlit, but once the votives inside them are alight they twinkle delightfully. They look especially atmospheric grouped together. Cut an assortment of fabric scraps into strips of different widths. Punch holes in some of the solid-colored fabric strips using a specialist hole-punch with a small hammer and cutting mat. Use double-sided tape on all four edges of each strip to stick it around a jar. Cut out some individual flowers from floral fabric, put small pieces of double-sided tape near the edges of the flowers, and stick these to some of the other jars. You could also spray paint the lids of the jars, and sit the jars on these.

place small candles or votives in the jars unlit, and then use long matches to light them. Be careful when picking them up when they are lit, as the glass may become hot, and remember never to leave lit candles or votives unattended.

display

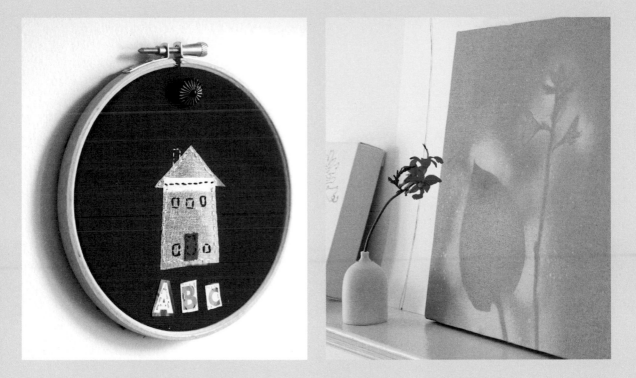

Even if you are intimidated by drawing, you will find
here a multitude of ideas for achieving a level of art in
your home that you are proud to have on show. Often
the frame is as important as the artwork inside it, and
the method of display becomes a work of art in itself.
In this chapter the two aspects are inseparable.

stitched portraits

These stitched portraits, created by machine stitching or hand sewing the outlines, make a great alternative to family photographs hanging on the wall. As the outlines are traced from real photographs, the pictures really can look like your family and friends, something that is hard to achieve with freehand drawing unless you are skilled at portraiture. You could also photograph favorite possessions or places, print them out, and treat them in the same way, as I have with a shoe. The best photos to use are those with clearly defined features and edges. Print out enlarged copies of them—these are easier to use than small images. The printouts can be either black and white or color and do not need to be of high quality. Bows and buttons can be stitched on the pictures at the end to add another dimension, as with the bow on the shoe.

materials and equipment

Computer printouts of photographs (see above)

Watercolor paper

Masking tape

Sewing machine or embroidery needle

Machine embroidery thread or stranded embroidery floss

Colored paper (optional)

Scissors

Ribbon or buttons, sewing thread to match, and sewing needle (optional)

machine-stitched portraits

1 Place each printout on top of a piece of watercolor paper that is larger than you need. Secure it with small pieces of masking tape at the top and the bottom. The printout will be removed and the paper trimmed, at the end. Thread the bobbin of the sewing machine with the same color as the top thread, put the embroidery foot on the machine, and set the machine to "darning."

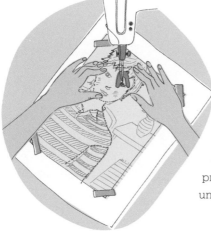

2 Put the taped layers of paper in the sewing machine. Begin to stitch, following the lines of the printout with your sewing machine needle, starting with the shape of the head and face. When you come to the eyes, you do not necessarily need to give the whole shape, just part of it—a concentration of stitches in one area can weaken the watercolor paper. Add the ears, hair, and shoulders, gradually building up the face shape and body. Check on your progress at intervals by turning the paper over and looking at the underside to see which areas still need work.

3 When you've stitched enough, remove the masking tape. Carefully tear off the printout to reveal the stitched portrait underneath. This can take quite a while if a lot of detail has been added. If you wish, leave a little of the printout in place—it will add depth and, if it is a color printout, it can add color to areas like the eyes and hair. Position the paper in the frame, trimming as necessary.

decorative variations

1 When making machine-stitched pictures, you could sandwich some colored paper between the printout and the watercolor paper in step 1, taping all three layers in place. Then, in step 3, tear off most of this colored layer, leaving it only in selected spots, such as the green hat shown here.

2 Another variation is to hand sew buttons, bows, or other decoration to the image after completing step 3.

hand-stitched portraits
- - - - - - - - - - - - - -

1 Attach the printout to the watercolor paper with masking tape all the way around, so that it won't slip while you are making the portrait. (Bear in mind, however, that you will need to be able to remove the tape at the end!)

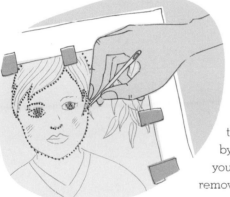

2 Using a pin or needle, carefully prick holes right through the printout and watercolor paper following the lines of the face on your photo. If possible, space them the right distance apart for you to embroider through in the next step. Check your progress at intervals by checking the underside of the watercolor paper. When you are happy with the outline of holes, take off the tape and remove the printout.

3 Using embroidery floss, sew backstitch (illustrated right) or running stitch along the lines of tiny holes, inserting the needle through the holes. For areas you want to be delicate (around the eyes, for example), separate the floss into individual strands and use just one or two strands. For areas you want to be thick, use the floss without separating it into strands. Fasten the ends of the floss on the underside of the paper by weaving it into the stitching, or tie small knots. Position the paper in the frame, trimming as necessary.

flower & leaf art

This project allows you to create pieces of art without having any drawing skills. The images work best when they include different plants and a variety of techniques. For delicate line drawings, all you do is draw around a real flower. Choose one with a simple shape, because the more complicated the shape, the harder it will be. For some of the drawings, fill in the outline with pen or paint. For more variety, create some leaf prints. Similarly, some of the flowers were simply placed on a canvas and then paint was sprayed over the top. I have always loved the work of the photographer Man Ray, who created negative images by placing unusual combinations of everyday objects on photographic paper which he then exposed to light. Your artwork could be taken in this direction by using objects such as keys, scissors, and buttons rather than the plants used here.

materials and equipment

Flower sprays and individual leaves

Paper or stretched fine-textured canvas in different sizes

Masking tape, pencil, and pen

Gouache paint and fine paintbrush (optional)

Newspaper and pebbles

Spray paint

Acrylic paint and ¾in (2cm) paintbrush

Small roller

line drawing

1 Pick a simple flower or leaf shape. If it still looks complicated when you lay it flat on your paper or canvas, then pick off a few buds, flowers, or leaves so the shapes don't overlap. If necessary, use a little masking tape to keep it flat.

2 Draw around the shape very carefully with a pencil (or a pen when you gain confidence), looking at every little lump and bump and recording it. When you have drawn around the entire shape, remove the flower or leaf slowly to see if the shape that is left is recognizable. You may need to cheat slightly by adding in a few lines to complete the shape. If you have used pencil, go over the outline with pen.

3 If desired, fill in the image using the pen, or gouache paint and a fine brush. (If you are creating a collection of artworks, fill in some of the outlines and leave others just as outlines.)

sprayed image

1 Choose a natural-colored canvas or piece of paper and a lighter spray paint, or a white canvas or piece of paper and a darker paint. Alternatively, you could paint the canvas a darker color and, when it is dry, use a light spray paint. Place the flower or leaf on the canvas and use a little rolled-up masking tape on the underside to hold it in position without being visible. The leaf or flower needs to be as flat as possible on the canvas or paper. Working in a well-ventilated space (ideally outdoors), put the canvas or paper on some newspaper (holding it in place with pebbles if outdoors).

2 Following the manufacturer's directions, start spraying the canvas or paper with the paint. Spray in gentle sweeps, not just in one spot or the paint will seep under the flower or leaf. Gradually build up the shape and color. The closer the leaf or flower is to the paper, the crisper the edge will be. If there is a space between the two, the line will be softer. You can use your fingers to keep the object as flat to the surface as possible, but it does mean you will have sprayed fingers!

3 After the paint has dried, slowly peel the stem away. If you can see the shape, enough paint has been applied. If you cannot, replace the stem in exactly the same position and build up another layer of paint.

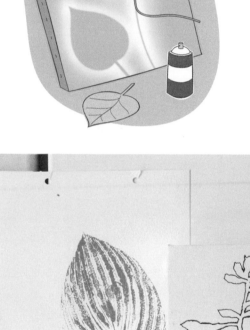

leaf print

1 Brush acrylic paint onto one side of the leaf with a ¾in (2cm) brush.

2 Place the leaf on the paper or canvas, paint side down, and apply even pressure over the whole leaf using a small roller. Carefully peel off the leaf to reveal the leaf print.

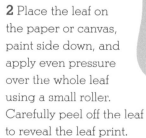

embroidery hoop pictures

Wooden embroidery hoops provide interesting and inexpensive frames for textile designs, whether used in their natural finish or painted. Even just a beautiful piece of fabric looks good stretched in a hoop, especially as part of a group. My inspiration for the designs shown here came from folk art and vintage embroidery samplers, with their alphabets and simple motifs. The small alphabet picture was made using a set of rubber stamps and ink, which I use all the time for gift cards and name badges. If you don't have a set of these, you could achieve a similar look by cutting out letters from a newspaper and sticking or sewing them on.

materials and equipment

Embroidery hoops

Scissors and pins

Linen in different colors

Iron and fusible web

Scraps of fabric

Pencil and paper (optional)

Embroidery needle and floss

Buttons, sewing needle, and thread

Cotton organdy, for Little House

Letters cut from newspaper or magazine, for Little House

Craft glue, for Little House (optional)

Ticking, denim, and scrap of polka-dot fabric, for Dog Cameo

Alphabet stamps and ink, for Stamped Alphabet

patchwork alphabet

1 Loosen the screw at the top of the hoop and separate the inner and outer circles of the hoop. Place on a flat surface. Using the hoop as a pattern, cut out a piece of linen ¾in (2cm) bigger than the hoop all the way around. Iron the linen circle and put to one side.

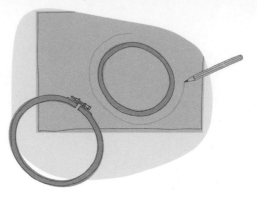

2 Following the manufacturer's directions, iron the fusible web onto the back of each fabric scrap you are using for letters. Cut out the letters from these scraps. I did them freehand, but you may want to draw the letters on a piece of paper first, cut them out, pin the paper letters onto the front of the fabric, and cut them out. (If you prefer to draw them on the backing paper of the fusible web, remember to do them backward, so that the fabric letters will be the right way around.)

3 Remove the backing paper from the letters and arrange them on a linen circle. You can now either iron them on or do as I did and simply pin and then sew them with a small running stitch, which accentuates the fact that they are handmade. (In that case, the purpose of the fusible web is not to stick them on but to provide a crisp edge and stop the fabric from raveling.) Or you can iron them on and embroider them. Small cross-stitches in the corners keep the letter "I" in place.

4 Lay the linen circle on top of the smaller ring of the embroidery hoop, making sure the fabric is centered, and then slide the larger hoop over it, with the screw at the top. Tighten the screw until the rings are held securely together and the fabric is taut. Cut off any excess fabric on the back of the frame once you are happy with the position of your artwork. Sew a button to the top.

little house

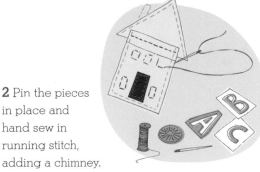

1 Cut out a dark linen circle as for the Patchwork Alphabet, step 1. Cut out three rectangles and a triangle for the house from fabric scraps. For the house and roof I used cotton organdy for its crispness and translucency, which is effective when the overlapping shapes show through.

2 Pin the pieces in place and hand sew in running stitch, adding a chimney. Use a contrasting color of floss to outline windows and the roofline. Roughly cut out letters from a newspaper or magazine and sew or glue them on. Complete as for step 4 of the Patchwork Alphabet.

dog cameo

Cut out a circle from ticking as for the Patchwork Alphabet, step 1. Also cut out a denim rectangle. Iron fusible web to the back of the denim rectangle and the back of a scrap of polka-dot fabric. Using the template on page 00, draw the Dalmatian shape on the backing paper of the polka-dot fabric, remembering that it will be backward, and then cut it out. Remove the backing paper from the Dalmatian, and iron it onto the denim rectangle. Now remove the backing paper from the denim and iron it onto the center of the ticking. Complete as for step 4 of the Patchwork Alphabet.

stamped alphabet

Cut out a piece of linen as for the Patchwork Alphabet, step 1. Stamp the letters onto the linen using a set of rubber stamps and ink, and leave to dry. If you wish, embroider inside some of the letters using running stitch. (Alternatively, cut out letters from a magazine or newspaper and stick or sew them on.) Complete as for step 4 of the Patchwork Alphabet.

linen bulletin board

This bulletin board has multiple uses. Because it is on display I wanted it to look attractive even without anything pinned on it, as well as being functional. I designed it to fit a specific space, and the colors of the bulletin board tie in with the shelves above it. The pins are made from counters from old board-games, such as Scrabble and Bingo, from which pieces had been lost or could be spared. The bulldog clips are great for invitations or items that are too thick or important to pin through, while paper and postcards can be tucked behind the ribbons. The pockets are handy for folded notes, receipts, and writing equipment, and like the bulldog clips they add splashes of bright color to the otherwise neutral tones.

materials and equipment

Linen, for base fabric	Staple gun
Corkboard or other type of bulletin board	Strong ribbon or twill tape in different colors
Long ruler, pencil or tailor's chalk, and scissors	Spray paint and newspaper
Swatches of fabric for pockets	Bulldog clips
Carpenter's square (set square)	Extra-strong multipurpose glue or two-part epoxy glue
Pins, needle, and thread	Counters from board games
Sewing machine (optional)	Flat-headed thumbtacks (drawing pins)

1 Press your linen base fabric, place it on a large flat surface, and lay the bulletin board on top. With a long ruler and pencil or tailor's chalk, draw around the board, allowing an extra 4in (10cm) all around, which will be folded over to the back of the board. Be careful to draw the lines exactly along the straight grain of the fabric. Cut out.

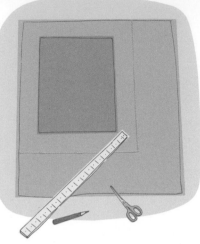

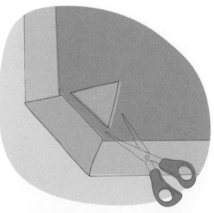

2 To make the pockets, mark out and cut rectangles from the fabric swatches, cutting them exactly on the straight grain. Fray the top edge of each pocket by using a pin to remove some of the threads parallel to the edge. Or if you prefer, turn under a double ¼in (5mm) hem on the top edge, and stitch. Turn under and press ¼in (5mm) along the side and bottom edges of the pockets. (Note: If you are using felt, suedette, or some other fabric that doesn't ravel, you do not need to turn under or fray the edges.)

3 Plan where the pockets should be positioned on the linen, taking into account the extra 4in (10cm) all around. Pin the pockets to the linen, making sure they are straight. Sew on either by hand using a small running stitch or by machine, stitching along both sides and the bottom edge.

4 With the fabric wrong side up, place the board face down on top of it. Start by folding in each corner and trimming off the triangle as shown.

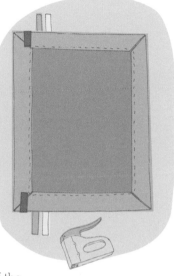

5 Starting in the center of one side and working outward to the edges, fold the linen border to the back of the board and staple it in place using a staple gun. At each corner, fold the fabric over with the corner still folded in, which will create a miter. Now do the same on the opposite side, pulling the fabric taut to make sure it is smooth. Finally, repeat for the remaining two sides. Staple over the mitered corners as well.

6 Place a length of ribbon or tape under the board, fold one end over to the back, and staple in place. Now fold the other end over to the back, making sure it is straight; pull it very tight and staple in place. If it is not taut enough, it will not be able to support anything and the objects will slip down. Repeat for the other two lengths of ribbon or tape.

7 If desired, spray-paint one side of the bulldog clips on some newspaper in a well-ventilated space, preferably outdoors. When the paint is dry, turn them over and spray the other side. When dry, clip them to the top of the board.

8 Glue the games counters to the tops of flat-headed thumbtacks (drawing pins).

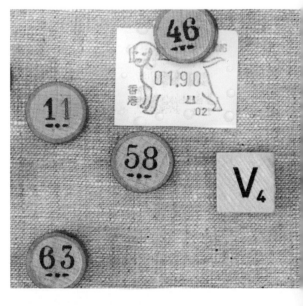

wired button decorations

Buttons make gorgeous decorations, which are all the more striking if used in unlikely places. Here I have wired them together to turn plain glass jars into pretty vases—perfect for low-key flowers such as daisies or buttercups—and to form delicate hearts to hang from a door knob or peg rail. The most economical source of buttons is to cut them off worn-out garments destined for the rag bag, and store them in a jar (decorated with buttons, of course!). My favorites from my own button jar are simple fabric-covered ones that my grandmother had given me. The notions (haberdashery) sections of department stores offer a wonderful selection of mostly inexpensive buttons that are just irresistible. Some buttons are so striking that they look good used individually.

materials and equipment

Glass jars

Wire

Wire cutters, or scissors if wire is thin

Buttons

jar decorations

1 Wash each jar and soak the label off. Cut a piece of wire long enough to twist around the rim and be secured firmly.

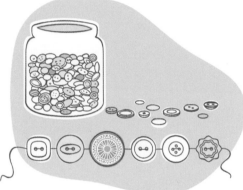

2 Tip out your button jar and select buttons that look good together. Thread the wire through the buttons. If they have shanks, give the wire a little twist at the back to keep the buttons in place.

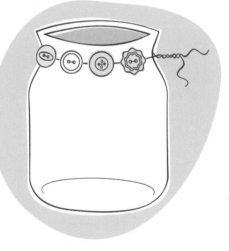

3 Pull the line of buttons out tight and wrap it around the neck of the jar, fastening the wire at the back with several twists.

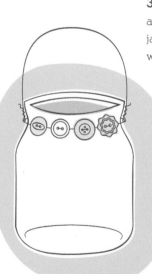

4 To add a handle, cut another piece of wire and wind each end through the encircling wire on opposite sides of the jar, twisting it to hold it in place securely. (If you wish, you could thread buttons onto the handle prior to attaching the second end.)

button hearts

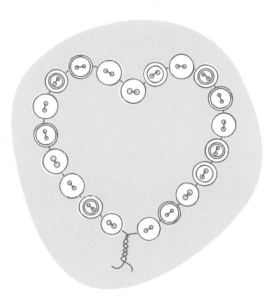

1 For the button hearts, select buttons that are roughly the same size. Cut a length of wire and thread it through them. Bend the wire into a heart shape, twist the ends together at the bottom, and hide them behind the buttons.

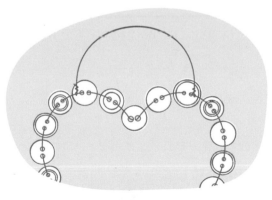

2 To add a handle, cut another piece of wire. Attach the ends to the peaks of the heart, twisting the ends to secure.

quick idea illustrated bunting

bunting is a timeless way to decorate a room, but this is bunting with a difference, because each triangle is decorated with a small illustration from an old book or with a postage stamp. Simply cut out a paper triangle to use as a pattern; 4–6in (10–15cm) deep is a good size, but you could incorporate more than one size if you wish. Use the pattern to cut out triangles from cotton organdy, and then machine stitch the paper illustrations or postage stamps to the organdy.

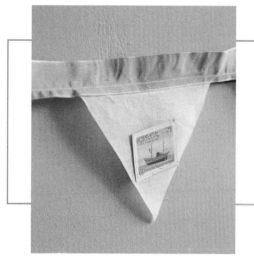

Pin the triangles to a length of ribbon, leaving at least 12in (30cm) of ribbon free at each end for hanging the bunting. Machine stitch all the way along the ribbon, stitching through the triangles. If you are making a lot of bunting, it will be easier to use if you make each ribbon no longer than about 5ft (1.5m), plus the amount left free at the ends for tying.

quick idea framed clothing

some children's clothes are just too precious to store or give away, so put them up on your wall to make lovely reminders of when your children were young. Children are always fascinated with their own baby clothes, as they cannot believe they were ever that small. Box frames are ideal for displaying clothing, as they will not flatten it. But you can also simply hang up clothing without any frame, or even stand an old frame in front of items mounted on the wall.

some of the woolens were items I shrank by mistake, and they had become felted after too hot a wash cycle. Rather than getting upset and throwing them out, I framed them for posterity. To make the insides more interesting I cut the existing labels out and made my own from patterned fabric, adding buttons as decoration.

for the ballet shoes I cut patterned fabric to the shape of the soles and sewed it in place with running stitch, but it could be placed inside without sewing. The brown shoes on the wall are so lightweight that they stay in place with putty-like adhesive; the polka-dot pants are also hung in this way. The white shirt has passed through three generations of my family, but was so well made that it survived my washing skills and still looks great.

quick idea painted frames

transform old picture frames

by painting and decorating them, then hang or stand them in a group to make an eye-catching feature. Start by painting them all with two or three coats of flat latex (emulsion) or satin eggshell paint in different colors, allowing it to dry between coats.

to disguise a cracked corner (as for the small green frame); find a scrap of floral fabric with motifs that can be cut out and used in the corner of the frame. Iron some fusible web onto the back of the fabric (to give a crisp edge that won't ravel), cut out the motifs, and stick them to the frame with double-sided tape.

to decorate a painted frame with fabric and ribbon, cut a strip of fabric to the circumference and length of the frame you wish to cover. Paint white glue onto that section of frame. Starting at the top, mold the fabric onto the frame, pressing it into the indents. At the top and bottom corners, cut the strip on the diagonal, following the line of the miter. Stick lengths of ribbon to the remaining sides of the frame using double-sided tape, cutting the ends to match the miters at the corners.

to make a cameo rosette for a frame, cut out a 4in (10cm) circle of thick fabric, and about nine 2¼ x 4¾in (5.5 x 12cm) strips of different fabrics. Pleat each strip and pin it around the circle, with the circle on top. Hand sew them in place with small, neat running stitches. Sew ribbons in different colors and lengths to the back of the rosette so they hang down side by side. Iron some fusible web to the back of a dark fabric, draw a silhouette of a head on the backing paper, and cut it out. Remove the backing paper and iron the silhouette onto the center of the circle. Press the pleats of the rosette flat. Finally, stick the rosette to the side of the frame with double-sided tape.

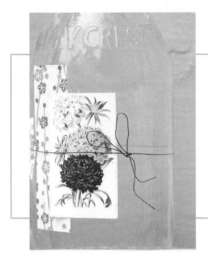

origami paper decorated with colorful traditional Japanese motifs looks great wired onto pretty glass bottles. The paper, which comes as flat squares ready for folding into origami shapes, is readily available and can be used for a variety of other craft projects.

to create deliberate clashes of color and pattern, try patching two together, as I've done on some of these bottles. You can also use other collected bits of paper in the same way, such as foreign food packaging, lace doilies, old photos, and scraps of wrapping paper.

choose bottles with interesting shapes, such as the chunky antique bottles included here, which had been dug up from a riverbed. You could even paint the bottle with a pattern to match the paper. Use a small piece of double-sided tape to hold the paper in place on the bottle, and then wind thin wire around it, twisting or knotting the ends of the wire. Use a funnel or small jug when filling the vases with water to avoid wetting the paper.

quick idea painted bottles

these stylish vases are made by painting glass bottles with a flat spray paint from a craft shop or with flat latex (emulsion), producing a lovely claylike finish. You can also use car spray paint, which gives a glossier finish resembling porcelain. I used tones of white, off-white, and cream for a sophisticated look, but other colors could look good, too. If you are using similar tones, choose bottles in different sizes and shapes to add variety to the grouping. For a variation, you could create a reverse-stencil effect by sticking on stripes, polka dots, squares, stars, or hearts in a pattern on the glass, spraying over them, and then removing the stuck-on shapes. After the paint is dry, leave them plain or draw simple grass shapes, stripes, or lettering on the surface using a pencil.

wash the bottles well, removing all the labels. When completely dry, either place them on newspaper on the ground outdoors (weighting the newspaper with stones at the corners) and carefully spray each bottle with paint, or use a medium-size brush to paint the bottles with three or four coats of flat latex (emulsion), allowing it to dry between coats.

quick idea tin can planters

this assortment of cans in different heights, widths, colors, and textures is the perfect foil for a selection of plants, as well as an excellent way to recycle. Some cans have decorative images that will look particularly bright and colorful. Wash the cans out well and turn them upside down on the grass. Use a screwdriver to pierce the base of each several times for drainage, being careful not to skewer yourself. Sand the rough edges inside, fill the cans with soil, and add your plants.

there you go—an easy way to make plant pots. If the cans go rusty after a while it will simply add to the patina. Remember not to place the cans on any surface that will be damaged by rust or water seeping through the drainage holes. Use an old saucer or plate to stand them on if necessary.

quick idea pots & pebbles

an easy and chic way to update your plant pots is to paint them with blackboard paint. You can then write messages or play games such as tic-tac-toe on the sides with chalk—the pots become a sketchbook that the rain cleans for you to begin afresh. You could also paint some of the pots to contrast with the blackboard paint—perhaps a bright shade or a sophisticated stone shade, which looks great with pebbles placed on top of the soil. If you come across any stones with holes in them, you could string them together, as here.

clean the outside of the pots and the inside rims thoroughly. Give the paint a really good stir, as it can go a little patchy if you don't. Apply two or three coats of paint to the outside and the inside rim, allowing it to dry between coats. Put some pebbles in the pots, add some soil, and then pot your plants. Decorate with pebbles or thick string.

gifts & other little things

The projects in this chapter are an irresistible mix of things you can give as gifts or make for yourself—they will all be well-loved, whoever is the lucky recipient! I always find that the best gifts are the things I am reluctant to part with, whether it is simple clothing and accessories or luxurious indulgences.

sewing bag with fabric corsage

This capacious bag makes a very useful gift. I use mine for sewing projects, but a larger version with wider handles could be used as a beach bag or a laundry bag. To be practical, the fabric needs to be sturdy, like the ticking I chose here. Denim or canvas would also be ideal, or you could make it from cotton for a slouchy effect, though it wouldn't be as strong. The design is simple, so it is quick and easy to make. The handles on this one are made from a tape measure, linking in with the bag's function as a sewing bag, but a strong ribbon would work well, too. The removable fabric corsage is easy to make and finishes it off nicely.

materials and equipment

Heavy fabric such as ticking, denim, or canvas

Tape measure and long ruler

Pencil and scissors

Iron

Pins, needle, and sewing thread

Sewing machine

Tape measure (made from fabric) or grosgrain ribbon, for handles

Buttons and ribbons

Fabric scraps, for corsage

Brooch back

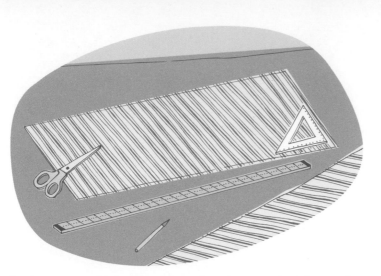

1 With a long ruler and pencil, mark and cut out the fabric to the desired size. The width should be the desired finished width plus 1¼in (3cm); and the length should be twice the desired finished length, plus 2½in (6cm). The finished size of this one is 20 x 20in (50 x 50cm), so I cut out a rectangle 21¼in (53cm) wide and 42½in (106cm) long.

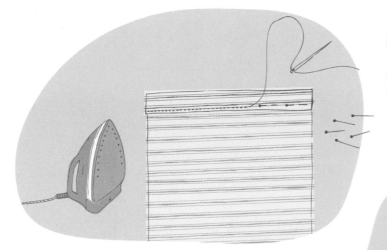

2 Turn under ¼in (5mm) and then 1in (2.5cm) at both ends; press and pin. Machine stitch in place close to the turned-under edge.

3 Fold the rectangle in half crosswise with right sides together and the ends even. Pin the raw edges together along both sides. Machine stitch ⅝in (1.5cm) seams. Press the seams open.

4 Cut the tape measure or grosgrain ribbon into two handles of the desired length. Pin the ends of the handles to the bag at the top. You can pin the ends to the outside as I have done, or to the inside. Similarly, you can either pin one end of a handle to the front and the other end to the back, as here, or pin both ends of one handle to the front and both ends of the other handle to the back.

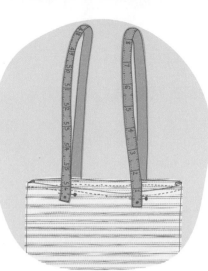

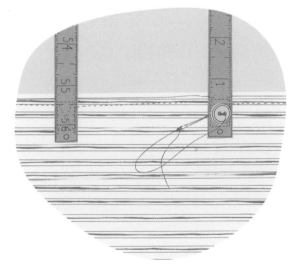

5 Machine stitch each handle to the bag. To do this securely, stitch across the end of one handle, up the side of the handle for ¾in (2cm), across to the other side, and back down to your starting point, and then stitch an X within this rectangle. Repeat for the other ends of the handles. Hand sew buttons, tags, or other embellishments in place, and tie on ribbons.

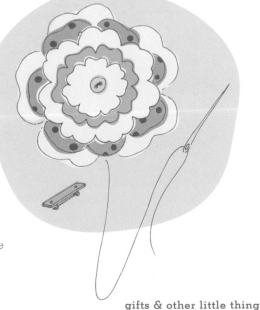

6 To make the brooch, use the templates on page 190 to cut five concentric flower shapes from paper. Use these paper patterns to cut out the shapes from the fabric scraps. Place the shapes on top of each other, graduating in size, with the largest at the bottom and the smallest on top. Hand sew them together. Sew the brooch back to the underside of the corsage through the holes in the brooch back. Sew a button to the top, and pin the corsage to your bag.

fabric-covered notebooks

Beautiful, fabric-covered notebooks are perfect gifts because they can be used as address books, diaries, scrapbooks, or places to write down favorite poems or quotations. Covered notebooks are expensive to buy but you can make them for next to nothing using plain notebooks and scraps of fabric. Old wallpaper could also be used instead of fabric. However, if the original notebook cover is dark or heavily patterned, make sure your fabric is thick enough that the original cover won't show through. Envelopes glued inside will hold receipts or mementos, while ribbons, tape, or leather strings can be used to tie the notebooks closed.

materials and equipment

Iron and spray starch

Fabric such as linen

Notebook

Pencil and ruler

Scissors

1in- (2.5cm-) wide double-sided tape

Needle and sewing thread

Button, ribbon, and large round sticker (all optional)

Twill tape or leather string (optional)

Craft glue (optional)

Fabric scraps, ribbons, or other decoration

Envelopes no larger than notebook

Paper (optional)

1 Iron the fabric with spray starch to stiffen it. Place the fabric wrong side up on your work surface and lay the notebook open on top. With a pencil and a ruler, mark out a rectangle on the fabric at least 1¼in (3cm) larger than the notebook all around. Using scissors, cut out the fabric.

2 Stick double-sided tape to the outside edges of the notebook, but not to the spine area as this needs to be free to move. Remove the backing paper from the tape. With the notebook closed, stick the fabric to the outside, leaving an equal amount of fabric projecting all around.

3 At each side of the spine at the top and bottom, snip into the fabric that projects beyond the notebook. Stick double-sided tape to the edge of the projecting fabric, but only as far as the snips—leave the fabric above and below the spine free of tape.

4 Remove the backing paper from the tape. Fold the taped fabric onto the inside of the book and stick down. Snip off the excess fabric at the top and bottom of the spine. Miter the corners as for the Linen Bulletin Board, steps 4 and 5 (pages 124–125).

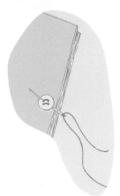

5 If you are using a button and ribbon, sew the button to the front, sewing through only the fabric by inserting the needle at an angle.

6 Cut the ribbon so it is long enough to be wrapped around the notebook at least once and then around the button (if used). If you have sewn on a button, stick the ribbon in place on the inside, just under the button, using a large round sticker. If you are not using a button, the ribbon doesn't need to be stuck on. If you are using a leather string or twill tape instead of ribbon, cut them so they are long enough to be wrapped around the notebook and tied. (If desired, you could make a tying loop at the end of the leather string, gluing the end in place.)

7 Stick on your chosen decoration. I used strips of colored polka dots and squares from a piece of fabric for one notebook, sticking them to the spine and front with double-sided tape. Ribbon looks pretty, too.

8 Stick envelopes to one or more of the pages with double-sided tape, leaving the flaps open to create pockets.

To cover the fabric edges on the inside of the covers, stick on either an envelope that is the exact size of the cover or a rectangle of paper or fabric cut to size. If you wish, make a bookmark from a strip of patterned fabric and place it inside. Tie the ribbon, leather string, or twill tape around the book.

lavender bags

Though simple to make, these are invariably popular presents because there is always room for one more in any closet or chest of drawers. They make clothes smell wonderful and are also a deterrent to moths. The starting point here was the ribbon, and I then matched the ribbon to fabric scraps from my stash at home. To add further interest, I decorated one bag with appliqué and hand embroidery and used an antique brooch from a charity shop to hold the ribbon together. As with the ribbon, very little fabric is needed to make these, and it's fun mixing and matching the colors. Square bags are the easiest shape to make, but a heart shape looks lovely hanging from a door knob or drawer pull.

materials and equipment

Carpenter's square (set square)

Pencil and paper

Scissors and pins

Fabric swatches at least 6in (15cm) square

Embroidery needle and floss

Fusible web and iron

Buttons and ribbons

Sewing machine and sewing thread

Sewing needle

Dried lavender

Small brooches

square lavender bags

1 Use a carpenter's square (set square) and pencil to draw a 6in (15cm) square on paper. Cut it out to use as a pattern. For a heart, use the template on page 189 to make a paper pattern. Pin the paper square or heart to your fabric and cut out two identical shapes for each bag. If you want to decorate the fabric with embroidery or appliqué, do it before stitching the bags together.

2 For the bird motif, first hand embroider the branch in running stitch on one dark square, using a light-colored floss. Iron some fusible web to the back of a fabric scrap that matches the floss, following the manufacturer's instructions. Using the template on page 189, draw the bird shape on the backing paper (remembering that the finished bird will be its mirror image) and cut it out. Iron the bird to the fabric square so it sits on the branch. Sew on a dark button for its eye, and a light-colored button for a moon.

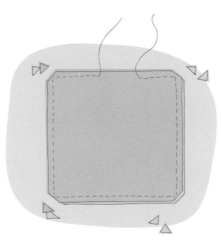

3 For each bag, place two fabric shapes with right sides together and raw edges even; pin. Machine stitch ¼in (5mm) seams around the edges, leaving an opening at least 2½in (6cm) long in one side. (To pivot at a corner or a point, stitch as far as the seam line of the next side, stop with the needle in the fabric, raise the presser foot, turn the fabric until the presser foot is parallel to the new side, lower the presser foot, and then continue stitching along the new seam line.) Snip off the seam allowances across the corners or points.

4 Turn the bag right side out through the opening, pushing out the corners or points; press. Make a funnel from paper and fill the bag with dried lavender through the opening in the seam.

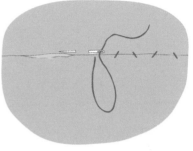

5 Turn in the raw edges, pin in place, and then slipstitch the opening closed using tiny stitches and matching sewing thread. Sew on any additional trimmings.

6 Make a few more square bags in the same way, using different colors. Stack them together, wrap ribbon around them, and either tie the ribbon or fasten it with a brooch. Cut each end of this ribbon into a "V" shape.

lavender heart

For the heart, use fusible web as in step 2 to attach a smaller heart in a contrasting fabric, then hand embroider running stitch just inside the edge of the smaller heart. Cut a length of ribbon and fold it in half to form a loop. Pin the loop to the right side of the heart, at top center, with the two ends together at the top and the folded end at the bottom. Complete the heart as for the square bags, steps 3–5. Pin a brooch to the heart next to the loop.

embroidered scarves

Practical and pretty, these scarves are perfect gifts. I made the pink one without the use of a sewing machine, one evening while sitting in the living room watching television. Even the edges were frayed and not machine stitched. The flower heads on it are made from buttons and the stems from running stitch, backstitch, chain stitch, and satin stitch. All stems and leaves could be created just from running stitch if you prefer, but using a variety of stitches adds interest to the design, and they are not difficult stitches to do. I made the beige scarf on the sewing machine using machine embroidery, with patches of fabric stitched on to form some of the leaves and flowers, augmented by some silk flower heads I bought.

materials and equipment

Soft fabric such as wool or wool mix

Tape measure, long ruler, and scissors

Pins and tailor's chalk

Pictures of flowers to copy

Also needed for hand-embroidered scarf:

Embroidery needle and floss in bright colors and several shades of green

Buttons

Also needed for machine-embroidered scarf:

Sewing machine with embroidery setting

Dark machine embroidery thread

Iron and fusible web

Scraps of patterned fabric

Small silk flowers (optional)

hand-embroidered scarf

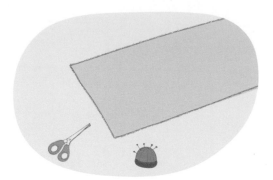

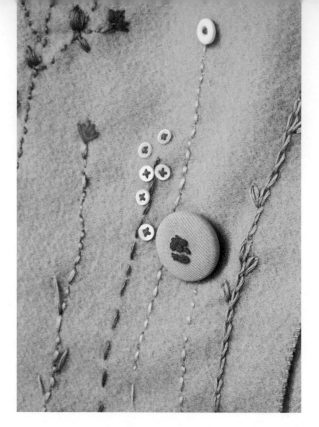

1 Cut out a length of fabric to the desired size—I made mine 70 x 10in (180 x 25cm)—cutting it exactly on the straight grain. Fray all four edges by using a pin to remove some of the threads parallel to the edge.

2 Referring to pictures of flowers, hand embroider floral shapes and stems. (If you prefer, lightly draw these first using tailor's chalk.) Start each stem at one end of the scarf, and embroider it as though it were growing partway up the scarf. Use backstitch (see page 113, step 3), running stitch (central stitch in illustration), and chain stitch (right-hand stitch). Embroider the leaves as you go, using chain stitch for some and satin stitch (left-hand stitch) for others. Add variety by using more strands of floss for some than others, in different shades of green. (Note: The illustration shows more than one needle to demonstrate how each stitch is done, but you obviously need only one.)

3 For some of the flower heads, use bright floss to sew on medium to large buttons or clusters of small buttons. Embroider other flower heads in bright colors of floss, using French knots, improvising your own using clusters of straight stitches, or using any of the stitches from step 2. You could also embroider French knots onto covered buttons.

machine-embroidered scarf

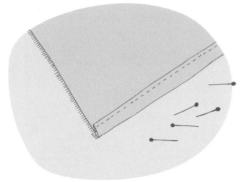

1 Cut out a length of fabric to the desired size—I made mine 70 x 10in (180 x 25cm)—cutting it exactly on the straight grain. Fray the short edges (see Hand-Embroidered Scarf, step 1). For the long edges, you can either fray them or turn under a narrow double hem on each and press, pin, and machine stitch it or zigzag the edge.

2 Set your sewing machine to "darning," put the embroidery foot on it, and thread it with a dark thread. Referring to pictures of flowers, machine embroider floral shapes and stems. (If you prefer, you can lightly draw these first using tailor's chalk.) Start each stem at one end of the scarf, and embroider it as though it were growing partway up the scarf. The technique is to "draw" each stem by moving the fabric around under the needle as it stitches. Create the leaves (some with veins, some without) as you go. At the top of some stems, stitch flower shapes, creating darker areas in the middle. Pull all the threads through to the back, and knot and trim them.

3 Iron fusible web to the wrong side of the floral fabric, and cut out some leaf shapes and flowers. Remove backing paper, pin on other stems, then machine embroider over them to hold them in place. Pull off the heads of any silk flowers you are using, and machine embroider them in place.

vintage sweater

This is a great way to save a sweater that has been attacked by moths or has holes in it, and you can also use it to liven up a simple sweater that just needs a lift. It works best if the fabric that you appliqué to the sweater has flowers or leaves that you can cut out as individual shapes. A geometric-patterned fabric would also work—little polka dots, for example, randomly arranged to cover any holes or marks would be fun. You could even make a skirt to match the appliquéd fabric. A finishing touch for the sweater is to embroider a personalized label (I made it from suedette, because it doesn't ravel), using your name or a special word that makes you smile every time you pull on your sweater.

materials and equipment

Old sweater

Fabric with motifs that can be cut out

Scissors and pins

Needle and sewing thread

Buttons and scrap of suedette

Sewing machine

Embroidery needle and floss (optional)

Darning mushroom or light bulb (optional)

Darning needle (optional)

1 Cut out the flower and leaf shapes from the patterned fabric, so that you have a pile of them ready to use. Position the cutout fabric flowers and leaves on your sweater, covering any holes and experimenting with different arrangements. I think they work best in little groups. When you are happy with how they look, pin them in position.

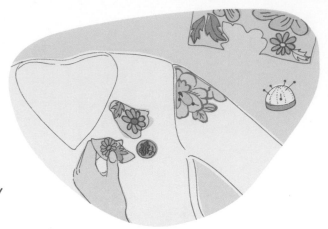

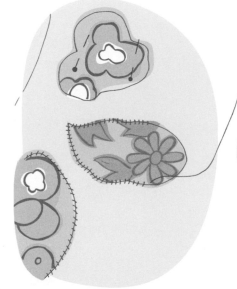

2 Hand sew the flowers and leaves to the sweater around the edges with tiny overhand stitches. Because the fabric edges are not turned under, the stitches need to be close together.

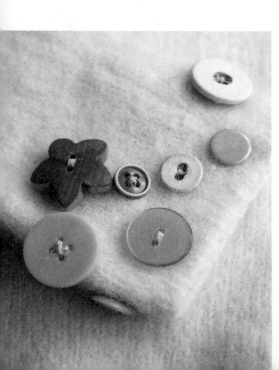

3 Choose a selection of interesting buttons that match the fabric flowers and leaves. I like them to be a little random in shape and size to add interest. Experiment with their positions, and then sew them on. You could use contrasting thread as an additional detail.

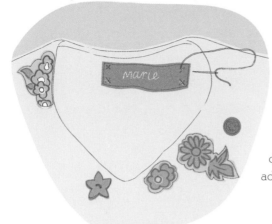

4 For the label, cut out a rectangle from the suedette. To machine stitch the name or word on the label, use the embroidery foot and the darning setting on your machine, and embroider the letters with straight stitch. Or, to hand embroider it, use small backstitches and just two or three strands of floss. Attach the label to the inside of the sweater at the center back of the neck using cross stitches at each corner. If you will be displaying the sweater rather than wearing it, you could add tiny buttons to decorate the label.

5 You could also darn some of the holes. (If you wish, use a darning mushroom or light bulb to provide a surface to stitch over, but be careful not to squeeze the light bulb tightly.) Either use a matching thread or go for a contrasting color to highlight the history of the garment. The aim is to recreate the missing fabric by weaving the stitches in rows. Thread the darning needle and tie a knot in the thread. Insert the needle from the wrong side and make parallel lines of running stitches that go beyond the hole by about ½in (12mm) all around. Take the stitches over the hole, too—they may have to be quite long. At the other side make a running stitch and then return in the same way. Continue doing parallel lines of running stitch until the hole is covered.

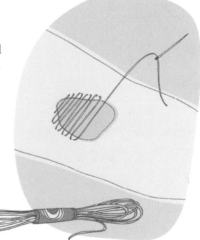

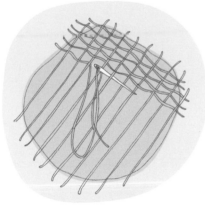

6 To complete the darning, weave the needle at right angles through the threads you have just made. Make a stitch at the end and then go back in the same way, but going over the threads you previously went under, and vice versa. Continue weaving parallel threads until the hole is eventually covered up.

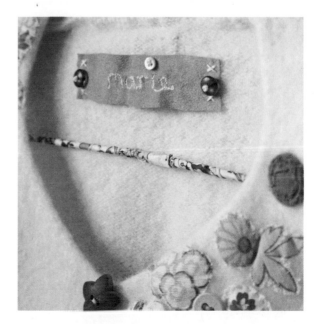

child's ribboned skirt

I made this pretty little skirt for my three-year-old daughter from an old curtain, which was among a pile of textiles donated to me by a friend. I felt that its charming old-fashioned quality was perfect for a simple little skirt. The buttons on the end of the ribbon, which is used as a tie, add decoration and also prevent the ribbon ties from disappearing inside the casing. The daisy trim around the bottom is in keeping with the nostalgic feel of the skirt.

materials and equipment

Iron and sewing machine

Old curtain or other fabric

Tape measure, long ruler, and tailor's chalk or pencil

Scissors and pins

Needle and sewing thread

Daisy trim or braid

Safety pin and 2¾yd (2.5m) ribbon ⅝in–¾in (1.5–2cm) wide

2 buttons, each ¾–1in (2–2.5cm) in diameter

1 If you are recycling an old curtain or other old fabric, wash and iron it well. Mark out and cut the fabric to size. I made this skirt to a cut length of 12in (30cm) for my three-year-old, which included an allowance of 2in (5cm) for a hem and a casing at the waist. However, check the length on the child it is for. The skirt will gather up when tied, so the cut width should be about 39–48in (100–122cm), depending on the weight of the fabric and the amount of fullness you want.

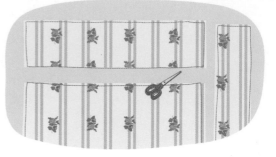

2 Now pin the two side edges with right sides together, and stitch a ⅝in (1.5cm) seam, leaving the top 2¼in (5.5cm) unstitched. Reinforce the stitching at the top end by stitching in reverse for a few stitches and then forward again for a few stitches. Press the seam open. Also press open the unstitched portion along the seam line.

3 Turn under ¼in (5mm) and then a further ½in (1.5cm) on the lower edge. Press, pin, and machine stitch close to the turned-under edge. When stitching over the thick side seam allowances, stitch slowly and carefully.

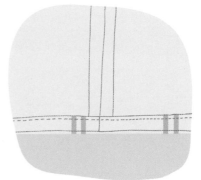

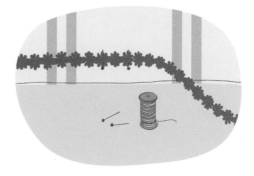

4 Pin daisy trim or braid along the lower edge, and stitch it in place.

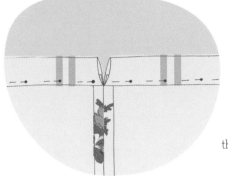

5 At the top edge, make sure the seam allowances on the unstitched part of the side seam are folded back (ie, wrong sides together) along the seam line. Turn under ¼in (5mm) and then a further 1in (2.5cm) on the top edge. Press, pin, and machine stitch close to the turned-under top edge, forming a casing. Once again, you'll need to stitch slowly and carefully over the side seam allowances.

6 Pin a safety pin through one end of the ribbon. Insert the safety pin through the open end of the casing at the top of the side seam. Work the safety pin through the casing until it comes out the other side. (If it gets stuck at the far end inside the turned-under seam allowance, ease the safety pin back, and maneuver it until it goes in between the two seam allowances and emerges from the casing.) Remove the safety pin.

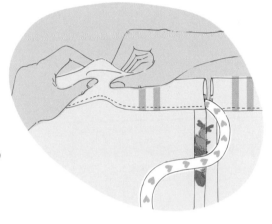

7 Turn under ¼in (5mm) at each end of the ribbon. Wrap a small piece of daisy trim or braid around the end of the ribbon, covering the turned-under end, with the ends of the trim or braid on the wrong side of the ribbon. Sew in place. Sew on a button at each end of the ribbon to prevent either of the ends from disappearing through the band.

8 Pin the ribbon securely in place at one end, and pull the other end to gather up the skirt. Ease the gathers along the top of the skirt until the whole waist is gathered up evenly. Undo the end of the ribbon that you pinned and pull it until it is roughly the same length as the other. Use these to tie the skirt when it is worn, adjusting the gathers to fit.

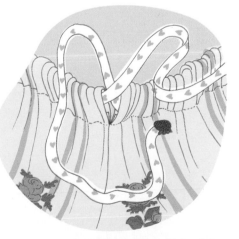

sock cats & dog

These little animals are a delight to make. Their personalities are impossible to predict before the sewing is complete, so there is bound to be lots of laughter as their funny little faces emerge. They were a great success with my children, who wanted to play with them the instant I showed them the animals. They also provide a perfect way to turn a mishap into a benefit—if a sock has disappeared in the wash or you felted your favorite wool socks by accident, you can turn them into gorgeous stuffed animals. If you don't already have a sock or two you can use, then buying a cheap pair will allow two animals to be made, and you can choose the colors or a pattern.

materials and equipment

Socks (one for each animal)

Batting (wadding) such as fiberfill

Sewing needle and thread

Scissors and pins

Fabric scraps (or the fingers cut from worn-out gloves)

Felt and ribbons

Sewing machine

Buttons and beads (optional)

Embroidery needle and stranded floss

Leather or suedette, for dog (optional)

Leather string, for dog (optional)

cat

1 The toe of the sock will be the cat's head. Fill the toe with batting (wadding) and wrap a piece of thread around the sock to form the neck, pulling it tight and knotting it securely. (Alternatively, you can hand sew with a double thread all the way around the neck in running stitch and then pull the thread tight and knot it.) For the body, stuff the rest of the sock with batting. Cut off any excess sock, turn under the raw edges, and pin and slipstitch the opening. You'll need to flatten out the bulge at the heel of the sock, so fold under the excess and hand sew in place using overhand stitch. If you don't do this, the cat will have a strangely large bottom!

2 For the legs and tail, cut out rectangles from fabric scraps or felt, measuring 3 x 2in (8 x 5cm) for each leg and 5 x 2in (13 x 5cm) for the tail. Pin the long edges and one end of each with right sides together, and machine stitch a narrow seam, rounding off the end. Snip off the corners of the seam allowance. Turn right side out and stuff each with batting, then turn in the raw edges at the end and slipstitch. Hand sew the legs and tail onto the body using overhand stitch. To use fingers cut from an old glove, simply stuff them, sew up the ends, and then sew onto the body as for fabric.

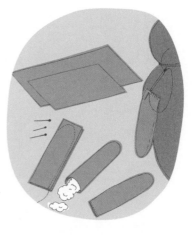

3 Sew on buttons as eyes and a nose, sewing them securely so they cannot be pulled off. If this is for a baby or a very young child, embroider them with French knots (see page 1600, step 3) instead. Embroider the mouth using small running stitches, and embroider claws on the paws using straight stitch.

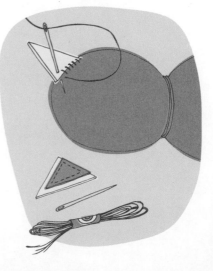

4 Ears like those on the pink cat and the pink-striped cat are made by cutting out felt triangles in two sizes and two colors. For each ear, place a smaller triangle on top of a larger one and sew them together using running stitch and floss. Now hand sew a pair of ears to the top of the cat's head using overhand stitch at the back of each ear. The fabric I used on the gray cat had lettering on the edge, which I incorporated in its ears, instead of adding smaller triangles, but its ears are otherwise the same as the other two cats'.

5 To make the whiskers, use all six strands of some white floss together. On one cheek make two stitches on top of each other, leaving long ends, and a loop between the stitches. Cut the loop in the middle and tie the two groups of floss in a knot on the cat. Cut the whiskers shorter if they are too long. Separate the strands to form the individual whiskers. Repeat on the other side of the face. Alternatively, embroider straight stitches on the face, as for the pink striped cat. Finally, tie a ribbon in a bow around the neck.

dog

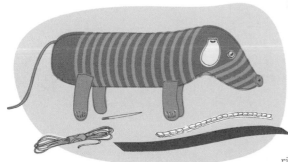

1 The toe of the sock will be the dog's rear end, and the heel will be the top of its head. Turn the sock wrong side out and with tailor's chalk draw a line as shown running from the back of the ankle of the sock down to the top of the toe. This will be the underside of the dog's snout, neck and belly. Pin along the line, leaving an opening of about 1½in (4cm) beneath the heel. Machine stitch along the pinned line on both sides of the opening. Trim away the excess, leaving a narrow seam allowance below the stitching line. Turn the sock right side out through the opening, and stuff with batting. Turn in the raw edges of the opening, pin, and slipstitch it closed.

2 Make legs as for the Cat, step 2, but don't slipstitch the ends. Turn under the raw edges and hand sew each leg to the body in two places, so that the inside of each leg is attached to the dog's belly and the outside of each leg to the lower part of the dog's side. Make sure that the feet are level so that the dog will stand up.

3 For the tail, sew a length of leather string or ribbon to the toe of the sock, near the top. On the dog's head, sew on buttons securely for the eyes and nose (or embroider them if the dog is for a baby or very young child—see the Cat, step 3). Cut out two ears in an elongated pear shape from felt, leather, or suedette, and hand sew the top of each ear near the top of the dog's head. Embroider claws at the outside front of each paw using embroidery floss. For the collar, wrap ribbon around the dog's neck and sew the ends together. If the dog is not for a young child, you can wrap a length of beads around the ribbon to make it look like a studded collar.

quick idea jewelry revamp

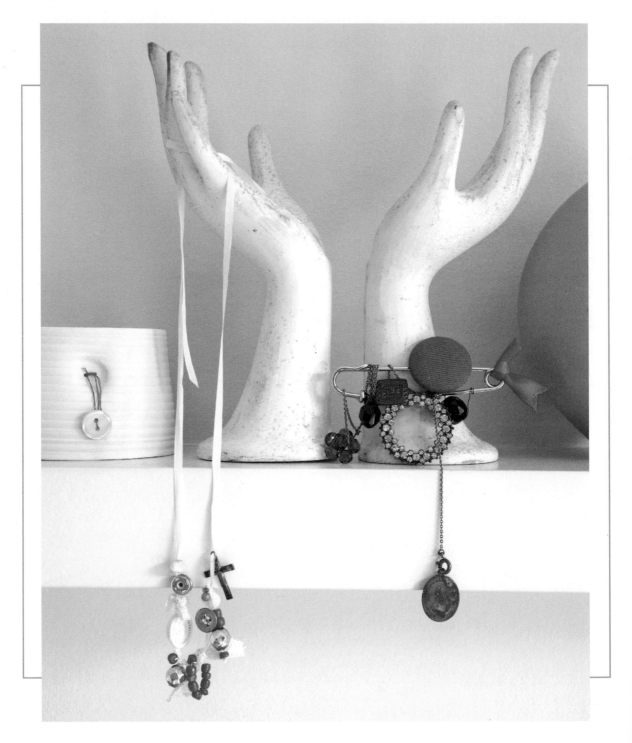

this striking jewelry, made from an assortment of beads, buttons, lace, and found objects, is guaranteed to be a talking point whether you wear it yourself or give it as a gift. It's also a great way to use pieces you haven't worn for years, broken necklaces, old chains, and other bits and pieces. To make this ribbon necklace, I rethreaded a broken coral necklace and sewed the loop onto a length of narrow ribbon. I did the same for some lovely buttons, and I tied tiny fragments of lace onto the ribbon where there were gaps. Finally, I threaded some snaps (poppers) and a cross onto the ribbon, which can be tied around the neck with a bow.

the kilt pin was embellished by wiring on a broken brooch and parts of a broken glass bead necklace. For the bead flower I threaded the center bead with wire, then threaded the wire through each bead, twisting it after, until they formed a flower, and finally twisted the wire at the top and tied it to the kilt pin. I also wrapped a chain around the kilt pin and tied it, and wired on a metal button and a covered button. For a splash of color I tied on a vivid piece of ribbon.

quick idea covered buttons

covering buttons in an unexpected fabric adds quirkiness and individuality to a garment. Use them to replace existing buttons—there's no need for them to match the garment or each other—or sew groups of them to the bottom of a sleeve or the shoulder of a jacket. Each button requires only a small scrap of fabric, so you can really go to town with your scrap bag and choose a great combination of different colors and patterns, or opt for a more coordinated theme.

covered-button kits are available, in which the buttons have tiny hooks on the underside and a disk that fits over the back, to hold the fabric in place. However, it's perfectly possible to cover existing buttons, so long as the buttons have a shank on the underside rather than holes in the middle. Cut out a circle with a diameter slightly less than twice the diameter of the button. Using a needle and strong thread, sew running stitch around the edge of the circle, leaving long thread ends. Place the button upside down in the center of the circle, and pull the threads to gather up the fabric circle around the button. Tie the ends of the thread in a tight knot. If desired, iron fusible web onto the wrong side of a contrasting fabric scrap, cut out a circle smaller than the button, remove the backing paper, and iron this circle to the front of the covered button.

quick idea polka-dot patches

these round patches look so good that you'll want to use them straightaway rather than waiting till holes appear in your sweaters or jeans. Use them simply to add interest to a plain garment, or utilize scraps from fabric used to make another garment that you then wear with this one.

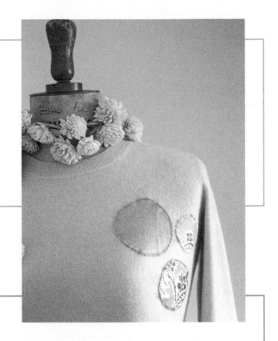

to make the patches, cut out fabric circles in different sizes. (If the fabric for the patches is thin, then also cut out larger squares from a backing fabric, and pin each circle to the center of a larger square, with both pieces right side up.) Set your sewing machine to zigzag with a ⅛in (2–3mm) stitch width and a very short stitch length, so the stitches are tight and solid. Zigzag around the edge of the circle, covering the raw edge. (If you have used a square underneath the circle, cut off the excess fabric outside the zigzagging, without cutting through the stitching.) Hand sew each patch to the garment using overhand stitch.

quick idea wrapped plants

wrapping fabric and ribbon

around a plant pot is a simple but effective way of smartening it up and transforming it into a special gift. The fabric can be low-key, like the linen I've used here, or more luxurious if you prefer. Muslin works well with natural string or twine wrapped around, creating a relaxed, understated look. Tailor the fabric and trimming to the plant and to the recipient—for example, you could tie the person's birthstone to the ribbon. As a final touch, make an envelope for the card to match the wrapping.

cut out a large enough circle of fabric to cover the pot, put the pot in the center, and bring it up around the pot. Ask someone to hold it in place while you wrap some ribbon around it and knot it at the back. Tie another bow, in a different color, at the front, and tie yet another ribbon around the center of this bow. Cut a V-shape into the center of each end of the ribbon. If the pot has tapered sides, make a few hand stitches with a needle and thread to attach the ribbon to the fabric.

to decorate with beads, thread them onto a length of thick embroidery floss; tie a large knot in the end so they won't slide off, and sew the thread to the center of the bow. (Note: If the pot has a hole in the bottom, don't water the plant after wrapping it.)

to decorate the envelope after inserting the card, wrap two ribbons around the envelope, and stick in place with a small amount of double-sided tape. Thread some beads onto wire, making a small loop at both ends (by threading the ends of the wire into the end beads) so the beads will not slide off. Bend the wire into the shape of the recipient's initial. Tie the initial to the wide ribbon using a piece of narrow ribbon.

quick idea collected treasure

this is such a lovely gift, not only because it is decorative but because it has a special meaning for the recipient. Everything on it—the name or initials, the date (a birthday, anniversary, or wedding day), a favorite color, and significant small items—can mean something to them, making it a keepsake that will always be treasured.

start with a box frame, and cut a piece of heavy watercolor paper to fit inside. Cut out capital and lower-case letters in different fonts from a newspaper to make up the person's name. Cut the numbers for the date from a tape measure. Sew buttons onto small fabric squares. Find appropriate small pieces of memorabilia, be it a charm from a bracelet, a broken brooch, a petal from the flower arrangement at a wedding, a photo, a cutout from a theater program, the paper from a fortune cookie, or a logo from a restaurant.

arrange all the elements to your satisfaction and glue them in place. Use adhesive pads for the items you want to be raised, cutting the pads into slivers so they are not visible. When sticking on the letters, you may need to use tweezers. Mount your handiwork in the box frame. If there are some items that are too large for it, place them on top of the frame or alongside. In fact, you could have as many items outside the frame as inside it!

quick idea herbal bath salts

preserving jars such as Mason (Kilner) jars decorated with ribbons and labels make a lovely way to give bath salts or potpourri as a present. I used dried lavender flowers or rose petals for these bath salts. To complete the gift you could wire a wooden spoon that has a hole in the top to the jar, to ladle out the salts, or you could slot a small vintage silver spoon into the front clasp or back hinge.

for the bath salts, fill a jar about two-thirds full with coarse sea salt granules (or a mixture of Epsom salts and sea salt). If desired, add several drops of lavender or rose essential oil, and stir really well. (Rose petals don't have as much scent as lavender flowers, so the fragrance from the essential oil is more important if you are using rose petals.)

top up with dried lavender or rose petals, and either stir to mix or leave them as they are, whichever you prefer. (Note: Whole rose petals look beautiful, but to avoid blocking the drain, it would be safer to crush them before adding them to the bath salts.)

wind a ribbon around the jar and tie the ribbon at the front with a bow, or just tie a bow around the fastening. Wire on a label, small beads, a large heart-shaped bead, a button, or a decoration of your choice. To make the metal house label, use a pencil to draw a house (including detail such as doors, windows, and a roof on the back of a metal craft sheet,

and cut out the shape with scissors. Pierce a hole in the top, thread through some ribbon or fine wire, and tie it to the jar.

Note: These bath salts could stain a plastic bathtub if not rinsed away thoroughly afterward. Also, they should not be used in a bath with jets, which could become blocked.

Templates

Apart from the butterfly templates on page 191, all templates are shown at the actual size used. The butterfly templates are shown at 50% of their actual size.

appliquéd table linen (bee and strawberry), page 12

appliquéd table linen (cake), page 12

appliquéd table linen (icing), page 12

appliquéd table linen (cake), page 12

appliquéd table linen (pot), page 12

leaf

leaf

placemat (flower)

placemat (flower)

placemat (flower)

appliqué pillow
(flower), page 46

appliqué pillow
(leaf), page 46

appliqué pillow (flower),
page 46

embroidery hoop pictures
(dog cameo), page 121

appliqué pillow
(leaf), page 46

appliqué pillow
(leaf), page 46

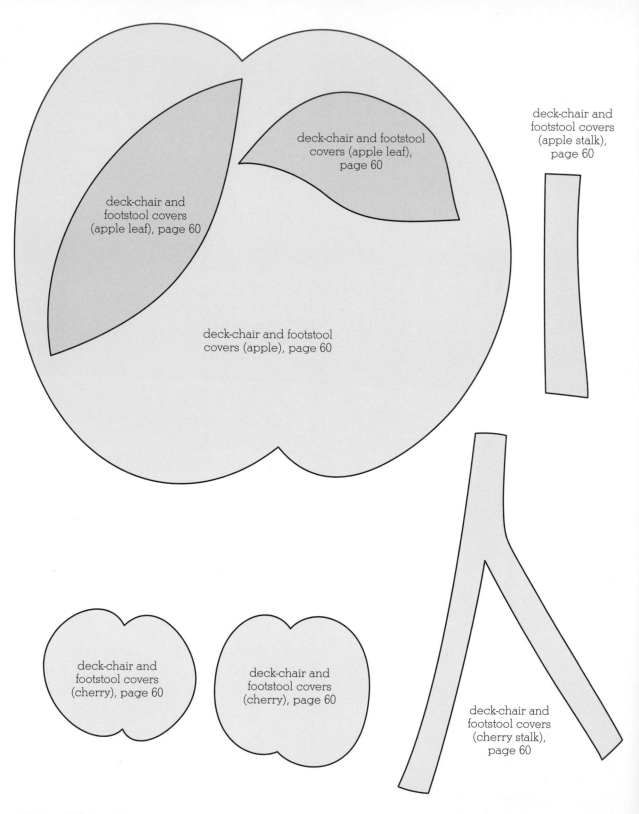

deck-chair and footstool covers (apple stalk), page 60

deck-chair and footstool covers (apple leaf), page 60

deck-chair and footstool covers (apple leaf), page 60

deck-chair and footstool covers (apple), page 60

deck-chair and footstool covers (cherry), page 60

deck-chair and footstool covers (cherry), page 60

deck-chair and footstool covers (cherry stalk), page 60

lavender heart,
page 154

stenciled
pillows (bird),
page 52

stenciled
pillows (bird),
page 52

sewing bag with
fabric corsage
(brooch), page 146

sewing bag with
fabric corsage
(brooch), page 146

sewing bag with
fabric corsage
(brooch), page 146

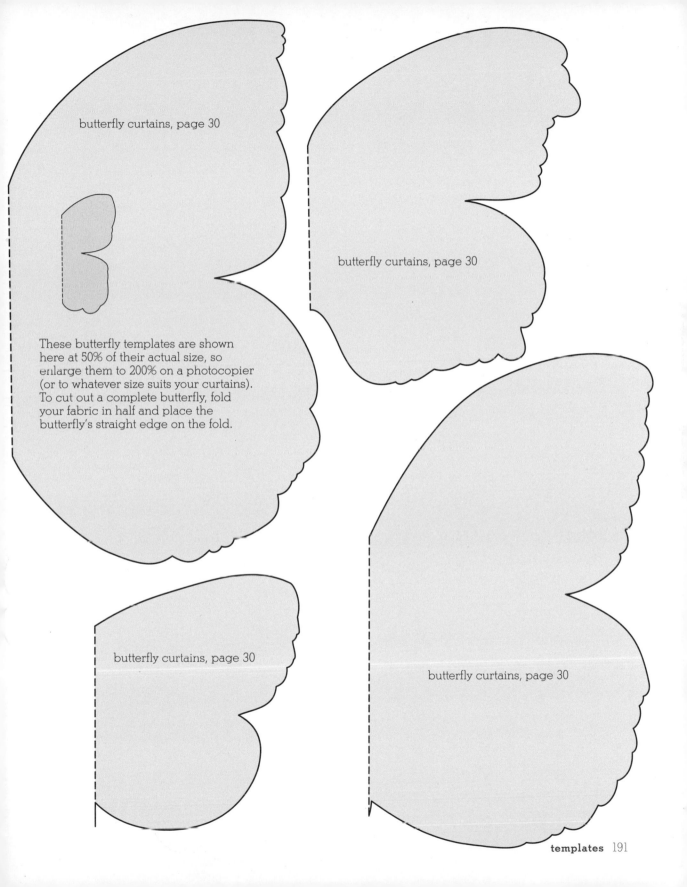

butterfly curtains, page 30

butterfly curtains, page 30

These butterfly templates are shown here at 50% of their actual size, so enlarge them to 200% on a photocopier (or to whatever size suits your curtains). To cut out a complete butterfly, fold your fabric in half and place the butterfly's straight edge on the fold.

butterfly curtains, page 30

butterfly curtains, page 30

Index

Author's acknowledgments

Thank you to my publishers Cico Books, and to Cindy
Richards for giving me this wonderful opportunity. To Gillian
Haslam and Alison Wormleighton for their careful editing. To
Sally Powell, without whose encouragement this book would
have remained an amalgamation of ideas on my computer
and in scribbly notebooks. To Penny Wincer for her beautiful
photography.

To my lovely friends and family who have helped look after my
children and lent or gave me materials with which to work.

To my parents who always encouraged me to develop my
creativity. And to my wonderful, creative family, husband, and
children, without whose support and understanding this book
would not have been possible. You make our house a home.

About the author

Sania Pell has a degree in textile design from Edinburgh
College of Art. After graduating, she worked for one of
London's top fashion and furnishing textile design studios
for seven years, where her designs were purchased by
companies such as Armani, Monsoon, Laura Ashley, Gap,
and Marks & Spencer. She then retrained as a stylist,
working for publications including Elle Decoration, The
Sunday Telegraph, and The Mail on Sunday and numerous
commercial clients. Married with two young children,
Sania lives in London. Her website is www.saniapell.com.